NEW TRENDS IN EDUCATION

By

Dr. S.K. Panneer Selvam

Lecturer

DPH

DISCOVERY PUBLISHING HOUSE PVT. LTD.

NEW DELHI-110 002

Published by:
Tilak Wasan

DISCOVERY PUBLISHING HOUSE PVT. LTD.
4831/24, Ansari Road, Prahlad Street
Darya Ganj, New Delhi-110002 (India)
Phone: +91-11-23279245, 43764432
Fax: +91-11-23253475
E-mail: parul.wasan@gmail.com
info@discoverypublishinggroup.com
web: www.discoverypublishinggroup.com

First Edition: **2011**
ISBN: 978-81-8356-804-3

New Trends in Education

Preface

The value of education is economic growth and development had not been recognized for a long time. The major problem confronting Indian education is the problem of compulsory primary education because the level of literacy has been very low. This shows that primary education has not expanded to the desired extent. Besides, many political, social, religious, economic and geographical factors are creating obstacles in the path of expanding primary education. This problem has been made even more complex by such contributory factors as the curriculum of primary education, problem of school, wastage and stagnation and many administrative difficulties. India is a pluralistic society comprising population of different socially disadvantaged sections and minorities.

These groups are different with each other as far as their life style, attitude towards education and other economic and social problems are concerned. Girls are forced an account of certain circumstances to leave education after a few years because of the prevalence of social evils of early marriage. Many girls and boys leave their studies at a premature age. This and many other social evils are responsible to a great extent for the prevalent wastage and stagnation, which is taking place in the field of education at different stage. India's economic and social structure is of a kind which encourages parents to send their children for general education.

Having thrust the entire burden of primary education on local bodies, the state Governments sleep the sleep of the just. But local bodies lack both finances and adequate means of raising resources and hence they also lack of enthusiasm for the spread of education. If the local bodies serve notices on the local population for the compulsory registration of children in schools, they cannot hope to obtain popular approval in elections. Besides, the presence of inefficient and neither of officials in the local administration further encourage stagnation. Besides, the presence schools are set up in an unplanned, haphazard manner, and this also adds to stagnation. In some areas, there are so many schools that the average attendance in them is only 100. Besides the inspecting staff is also over-burned as it is expected to make a survey of 100 schools every year.

The universalization of primary education could be achieved only if any measure will take to investigate the 5.75 lakhs of children. The Government has started District Primary Education Programme (DPEP–1984) Sarva Siksha Abiya (SSA, 2003) have recently started only with aim of providing equal education opportunities irrespective of caste, religion and so on. Even cent percent enrolment of drop-outs is not possible even thought there are so many attractive schemes like free books, free cloths, free and mid day meals, continent time schedule focusing on vocational skills and so on. As the investigator being a teacher education is SSA, he was stimulated much on how the special school children get education equally like other children. Dr. A.P.J. Abdul Kalam has pointed out that our educational system should develop certain capacities like inquiry, creativity entrepreneurial and moral leadership in the learners, so that they will be able to face the facilitate there participation in the task of national development. Information and communication technology has brought many ways to develop these capacities. Hence the teachers should be competent enough to conduct and facilitate learning through the recent developments in technology.

Educational Technology implies a behavioral science approach to teaching and learning in make use of pertinent scientific and technological methods and concepts developed in psychology, sociology, communications, linguistics and other related fields. Educational technology is the development, application and evaluation of system, techniques and aids to improve the purpose of human learning. Educational Technology should help to improve the overall efficiency of the learning and teaching process. Technology in education has seen many successes. It is the ingenuity of teachers who saw great potential in various technologies and adopted them to their advantages. Technology is meant to help as excel in whatever we are doing, improving our efficiency even make out life easier perhaps.

In order to bring effective improvement in the quality of education it is necessary to focus attention on the new technologies. One such recent and most dominating technology is computer technology computer plays great revolution in every walk of life. But when we think about its development in the field of education it is only in an infant stage. Now many people start thinking to add computer education in curriculum at all possible ways.

Dr. S.K. Panneerselvam

Contents

ACADEMIC AND ECONOMIC FACTORS

Chapter 1

Introduction

Education has a tremendous potential to function as an instrument of social change. In fact, it has been put to such use in several parts of the world.

EDUCATION AND SOCIAL CHANGE

What is the role of education in social change? How can formal and non-formal systems of education be used to bring about social change? In particular, what is the role of teacher in social change? Are they agents of social change or leaders of the process?

These are all questions that teachers need to answer for themselves.

EDUCATION—ECONOMIC GROWTH AND DEVELOPMENT

The value of education in economic growth and development had not been recognised for a long time. *Robert Bald and Gerald Meler* reports that "since the mid eighteenth century, economists devoted a large proportion of their labours to the subject of economic development, but only a small fraction of these studies include non-economic variables and these few works are scattered through the mainstream of economic thought.

In fact *Dension* in his analysis of economic growth in the United States arrived at the conclusion that though, between 1909-29 the economic growth in the United States may be traced to the influence of economic factors still the growth during 1929-1957 was more due to education and related non-economic facts than physical capital. The following table which gives a comparison of the GDP, per capita GDP and literacy figures for some of the developed and developing countries of the world highlights and the value of education in development.

Name of the Country	GDP in Million*	GDP Per Capita	% of Literacy**
Developed Countries			
United States	1060318	5121	100
United Kingdom	136392	2454	100
Japan	229809	196	100
France	162697	3175	100
(1971 data at current prices)			
Developing Countries			
India	57320	104	31
Indonesia	13957	118	39
Pakistan	11185	204	19
Burma (Myanmar)	2135	79	58
Srilanka	22333	176	75
Thailand	6988	198	68
Brazil	32169	349	76.7
Chile	6124	640	76.7
Jigeria	5310	99	26.3
Ghana	1887	221	26.3
(1969 data current prices)			

* GDP and Per Capita figures and from UN Statistical Year Book, 1973 For All Countries, pp. 596-598.

** Percentage of Literacy, Economic Survey of the Asia and the Far East, 1972, Unpulications, pp.65.

The table enclosed is very clear. It does not need any explanation. It shows that developed countries have cent per cent literacy rates. The value of literate and informal population for economical growth and development needs no further testimony.

STATEMENT OF THE PROBLEM

Article 28 states parties recognise the right of the child to educational progressively and on the basis of equal opportunity, they shall in particular: make primary education compulsory and available free to all. Moreover article 45 reports the provision of free compulsory education up to the age of fourteen. From the perusal of the above two articles, it is proved that every child is having right to get education at least elementary education. But majority of economically backward parents are not aware of this and carp the rights of the children by way of sending them for job. But looking from the angle of drop-outs children it is interesting to note what themselves feel on certain factors like Academic, Economic and Social factors.

Problem of Primary and Compulsory Education

The major problems confronting Indian education is the problem of compulsory primary education because the level of literacy has been very low. This shows that primary education has not expanded to the desired extent. Besides, many political, social, religious, economic and geographical factors are creating obstacles in the path of expanding primary education. This problem has been made even more complex by such contributory factors as the curriculum of primary education, problem of school, wastage and stagnation and many administrative difficulties.

DEFINITION FOR KEY TERMS

The important terms in the statement of the problems are drop-outs, Academic factor, Economic factor and Social factor.

Drop-outs : Drop-outs are a universal phenomenon which varies from country to country and from region to region with in the same country. A student may attend a course of study for its prescribed duration but:

(*i*) May not appear at the examination and discontinue the studies;

(*ii*) May appear and fail in any one of the examination and discontinue the education;

(*iii*) May appear, pass but discontinue further study.

The drop-outs not only betray the ambitions of the parents but also prove to be a great wastage of their money, time, efforts and resources of the government which in turn is a great set-back for the nation.

Academic Factor: The school itself appears related to drop-out rates, Schools with rigid retention policies, widespread administrative transfers, emphasis on competency testing, tracking and perceived 'unfair' discipline practices tend to have higher drop-out rates. Large class size, high teacher turnover, low teacher expectations for student performance, and perceived lack of support for students with academic and behaviour problems is also related to student decisions to drop-out.

Economic Factor : Number of children in the family, absence of a parent, lack of reading material in the home, parent's education level and families socio-economic system are also related to students decisions to dropout.

Social Factor : India is a pluralistic society comprising population of different socially disadvantaged sections and minorities. These groups are different with each other as far as their life style, attitude towards education and other economic and social problems are concerned. Girls are forced an account of certain circumstances to leave education after a few years because of the prevalence of social evils of early marriage. Many girls and boys leave their studies at a premature age. This and many other social evils are responsible to a great extent for the prevalent wastage and stagnation, which is taking place in the field of education at different stage.

STAGNATION AND WASTAGES

It was stated in the Hertog Report that the term stagnation was taken to mean keeping a child in one class for more than one year. R.V.Parulkar has explained that schools are established to provide education to children, and not to fail them. No other words, stagnation means the continuance of a child in a single class for two or three years due to failure. This to involve wastage of man's ability and the nation's energy, resources and manpower.

Besides, failure encourages a sense of inferiority in the child, and when children younger than him become his classmates, his abnormality tends to increase. Every year, the level of stagnation in primary classes in between 30 per cent and 50 per cent.

Causes of Wastage

Single Teacher Schools: Schools with single teachers make a special contribution to wastage. According to the report of the Indian Survey, these schools have played a significant role in this matter. It is difficult for a single teacher to handle five classes simultaneously. If he goes on leave, the school closes down. This makes the students reluctant in going to school and soon they drop-out altogether.

Socio-economic Structure : India's economic and social structure is of a kind which encourages parents to send their children for general education. Even today, our rural population holds on to the belief that a child should only be educated to the extent of being able to read and write.

The Child as Labourer : Children living in villages are the property of their parents who can compel their children to labour and earn on the fields. For such parents, the money earned the child is more important than his education.

Schools Without Resources: Many schools are almost completely lacking in the resource necessary for teaching and in the absence of these means, the teacher cannot teach. Consequently, the children engage themselves in playing here and there and in the absence of satisfactory results soon leave the school.

Lack of Space in Schools: Wastage also occurs in schools which have only make shift arrangements for housing the children.

Causes of Stagnation

Inefficient Administration: Having thrust the entire burden of primary education on local bodies, the state Governments sleep the sleep of the just. But local bodies lack both finances and adequate means of raising resources and hence they also lack of enthusiasm for the spread of education. If the local bodies serve notices on the local population for the compulsory registration of children in schools, they cannot hope to obtain popular approval in elections. Besides, the presence of inefficient and neither of officials in the local administration further encourage stagnation. Besides, the presence schools are set up in an unplanned, haphazard manner, and this also adds to stagnation. In some areas, there are so many schools that the average attendance in them is only 100. Besides the inspecting staff is also over-burned as it is expected to make a survey of 100 schools every year.

Lack of Money: The main stumbling block is the lack of finance. Local administration cannot spend adequate sums on education. In order to obtain grants from the State Governments, it has to live at the mercy of the Government. Because of this, there are difficulties in arranging not only the salaries of teachers, but even the materials needed for teaching.

Social and Religions Problem: Social and religions problem also contribute to stagnation. In schools which have a dominance of children belonging to a particular caste, tribe or group—such as tribal, scheduled castes, minority language groups, etc., other groups are neglected and this itself becomes the cause of stagnation.

Physical Facilities: The high percentage of stagnation is also accounted for the fact that, from the educational view point, rural areas, hilly regions and forest regions are neglected.

Educational and Economic Factors: Low standards of teaching, inadequate and unsuitable curriculum, the poverty of the people, etc., are also factors in stagnation. The two later factors help to a very great extent, in lowering the standard of education.

Stagnation and Wastage—The Kothari Commission: The Kothari's Education Commission has identified the following causes of wastage and stagnation:

1. The existence of discrimination between children of different ages in a class;
2. The admission of children to classes throughout the year, while this should occur at fixed time only;
3. The irregularity in attending school;
4. Absence of adequate teaching aids and minerals both with the schools and the students themselves;
5. Excessive number of students in classes;
6. The curriculum not being in conformity with needs;
7. The absence of ability and capacity in the teacher to teach through play thus depriving school life of joy.

Removal of Wastage of Stagnation

- The various sources of human development should be developed.
- Efforts should be made to discover how the best form of educational development can become possible.

- There should be planning to ensure that the right kind and quantity of education is made available to every person.
- Suitable traits should be generated for the development ability.
- The power to provide facilities should be generated.
- Manpower should be utilised suitability.
- Vocational and professional education should be developed.
- The Education Commission's concept of life-long education should be followed.
- A clearly defined national educational policy should be framed.
- There should be rigorous control over schools.
- The curriculum should be reformed and made useful for life.
- Arrangements should be made for the training of teachers.
- Laws should provide punishment for the training of teachers.
- Audit education should be extended. Education for girls should be expanded.
- 50 per cent of the total educational budget should be spent on primary education.
- Classes 1 to 4 should be regarded as a unit.
- Local cess should be imposed for financing education.
- There should be uniformity in education throughout the country.

The Education Committee has clarified that there should be overlooking the fact that wastage and stagnation are not illness like headache and fever, but the symptoms of other diseases concealed in the educational method. Of these the main are lack of proper harmony between education and life, and the defective management of schools which fails to attract the students towards the school. Wastage and stagnation are not, in themselves problems. In fact, it is a process, the sources of which whose selfish interests have blinded them to reality. There is no need to solve the problem of wastage and stagnation. What is actually needed is a change in the nature of its source so that these symptoms of a deep malaise may disappear and every child may be able to make his own contribution to the development of the nation.

Period of the Study

The period of the study was five years from 2001-2005.

NEED FOR THE STUDY

The universalisation of the primary education in India is the one of the recommendations of national Policy on Education. There is no doubt the majority of children are completing school education through formal education system. Around six lakhs child labourers are in Tamil Nadu (State Pattern of the Project 2003). At the same time the remaining 5.75 lakhs children are yet to be educated.

The universalisation of primary education could be achieved only if any measure will take to investigate the 5.75 lakhs of children. The Government has started District Primary Education Programme (DPEP-1984) Sarva Siksha Abiyan (SSA, 2003) have recently started only with aim of providing equal education opportunities irrespective of caste, religion and so on. Even cent per cent enrolment of drop-outs is not possible even thought there are so many attractive schemes like free books, free cloths, free and mid-day meals, continent time schedule focussing on vocational skills and so on. As the investigator being a teacher education in SSA, he was stimulated much on how the special school children get education equally like other children.

The investigator wanted to probe the attitude of the drop-outs children towards themselves and other concepts like Academic, Economic and Social factors. Hence the problem is stated as Influences of Academic, Economic and Social factors for drop-outs.

CONCLUSION

The dissertation has been organised in six chapters. Chapter I—Introductory part of the thesis deals with conceptual framework different nature of drop-outs children, statement of problem, differentiation of key terms, significance of the study and need for the study. Chapter II—Review of related studies concentrates on attitude and other related areas of special education of both published and unpublished researchers done in India and abroad are discussed. Chapter III—Profile of the study area. Chapter IV—Methodology provides design of the study, the details of the selection and size of the sample sampling technique, tool used. Data collection, statistics used for the data analysis with respect to variables such as sex, community, drop-outs willing and non-willing to go to school and drop-outs engaging in nature of the work. Chapter—VI Summary and findings deals with summary implication of the study, recommendation for the study based on the present study in detail.

Review of Literature

Chapter 2

INTRODUCTION

A review of related literature pertaining to the problem under investigation is a fundamental importance of the research. The research needs to acquire up-to-date information about what he has thought from which he is interested to take up a research problem. For any worthwhile he is interested to take up a research problem. For any worthwhile study in any field knowledge, the researcher needs adequate familiarity wish the literacy and its resources; only then there will be achievement of an effective search for specialised knowledge is possible. Though a time consuming process, review for related literature is a very fruitful process for research programme. Every investigator must know what sources are available in the field of enquiry which of them.

According to *Best (1977)* "A brief summary of previous research and the writings of recognised is a familiar wish what is already known and wish what is still unknown and untested. This step helps to eliminate the duplication of what has been done and provides useful hypotheses and helpful suggestions for significant investigation."

CLASSIFICATION OF THE STUDY

The investigator located 33 studies as related studies. Out

of studies 26 studies were conducted in our country and 7 studies were conducted abroad.

SIGNIFICANCE OF THE RELATED LITERATURE

Research takes the advantage of the knowledge which was accumulated in the past as a result of constant human endeavour. It can never be undertaken in isolation of the work that has already been done on the problems which are directly related to a study proposed by researcher. A careful review of the research journals, books, dissertations, theses, and other sources of information on the problem to be investigated are one of the important steps in the planning of any research study. Review of the related literature, serves the following specific purposes:

(*i*) A careful review helps the researcher in selecting the variables lying within the scope of his interest, in defining and operational zing variables and in identifying variables which are conceptually and practically important.

(*ii*) It helps the researcher in avoiding any duplication of work done earlier, specifically when the stability and validity of its results have been clearly established.

(*iii*) It also gives the researcher an understanding of the research methodology which refers to the way, the study is to be conducted.

(*iv*) The review of the related literature helps the researcher to know about the tools and instruments which proves to be useful and promising in the previous studies.

(*v*) The advantage of the related literature is also to provide insight into statistical methods through which the validity of research is to establish.

(vi) The final and important specific reason for reviewing the related literature is to know about the recommendations of previous researchers for further research which they have listed in their studies.

Studies on Cognitive and Non-cognitive Factors

Bombay Municipal Corporation (1967) conducted a study of the incidence of wastage and stagnation and the effectiveness of our educational efforts. The objectives of the study were to determine the extent of wastage and stagnation in primary schools, the reasons for it and their relation to the age of the children. About 6400 children were selected as the sample of the study from seventeen schools from year 1950 to 1958. Major findings of the study revealed that: (1) the percentage of children who left school fell from 43.3 to 21.4 in the year 1956 to 1958; (2) 92.9 per cent children left school after one failure in 1957 as against 49.7 per cent in 1950 and 3.46 per cent left school, after passing as against 6.51 per cent.

Sharma, R.C and Sapra C.L. (1969) carried out an investigation of wastage and stagnation in primary and middle schools in India. The aim of the study was the problem of wastage and stagnation in depth and to ascertain and analyse and stagnation in depth and to ascertain and analyse the cause of it. A sample of 790 drop-outs and 485 stay in cases was selected from 92 schools, school information blanks, pupil information sheets, and interview schedules were the tools of the study. Information findings of the study revealed that: (1) wastage and stagnation was 65 per cent at primary level and 78 per cent at elementary level; (2) About 50 per cent if wastage was noticed in class I itself; (3) The rate of drop-out is negatively related to the qualification and the preoccupation in case of teachers; (4) Drop-outs were usually from nuclear families who suffered the death of one or both parents.

Das, R.C. (1969) conducted a study of the wastage and stagnation at the elementary level of education in the state of Assam. The main objective of the study was to study wastage and stagnation with special reference to primary the study. The study revealed the following results: (1) Inspire of a rapid increase in educational expenditure, efforts and facilities, the rates of wastage and stagnation were 77.12 per cent at primary and 38.45 percent at middle level for pupils of general; (2) The rate of stagnation among girls was higher than that of boys.

Barua, A.P. (1971) studied wastage in Sibsagar and Golghat sub-division. The major objective of the study was to compare the wastage and stagnation at the primary stage during a period of five years. A twenty per cent systematic random sample was drawn which included 113 schools with 2342 pupils from Golghat sub Division and 151 schools with 2872 pupils from Sibsagar Sub Division. Major findings of the study revealed that: (1) The wastage at primary stage for boys and girls in Golghat Sub-division was 80.38 and 78.39 per cent respectively. In sibsagar sub division, the wastage for boys and girls was 70.08 and 69.02 per cent respectively; (2) The level of educational wastage was affected by three factors, *viz,* drop-outs, stagnated and transfer cases; (3) Poverty, ignorance of parents, poor health of pupils, repeated failure and bad physical conditions of the school were the main factors responsible for the wastage.

Khandekar, M (1974) conducted a study of drop-outs. The major objectives of the study were to find out the socio-economic and environmental characteristics of drop-outs and to determine their motivation fot further education and vocational training. The sample of the study consisted of drop-outs in the age groups of fourteen to twenty-one years. The investigation revealed that: (*i*) more girls than boys stopped education due to non-economic reasons; (*ii*) sixty-nine per cent of drop-outs stopped in their parents; (*iii*) Financial resources were the main causal factors; and (*iv*) fifty-two per cent of drop-out wished to start education again; (*v*) Quit a few drop-outs had high job aspiration.

Gupta, S.L. (1974) conducted a study of the impact of the un-graded school system on reducing school drop-outs and stagnation in primary schools. The main objective was to see the impact of un-graded school system on reducing school drop-outs and stagnation in primary schools survey method was used for the collection of data. Progress on tests and interviews were the tools. Findings of the study concluded: (1) The drop-out rates for the experimental group, for the project period was 31.7 per cent as against the average of 57 per cent; (2) The average daily attendance and the levels of achievement of the project pupils were higher; (3). The additional cost involved in the upgraded system was only 1.26 per pupil per year and hence negligible.

Punalekar, S.P. (1975) conducted a study of school drop-out among Harijan children, causes and cure. The chief aims of the study were to study the socio-economic background of the drop-outs and to identify the lapses or shortcoming on the part of the Harijan families, school system and village community. 198 drop-outs and their parents were interviewed as the sample of the study. Findings of the study highlighted the following major points: (1) The monthly income of 78 per cent families was Rs. 200 or less; (2) 80 per cent children attended school regularly and one fourth regularly attended to home work; (3) The main reasons for their dropping out were the economic hardship of the family, ill health in the family or of the child; (4) In 70 per cent cases the decision to drop-out was taken by the family while in remaining cases it was by the child; (5) The drop-outs had low aspiration level.

Masavi, M. (1976) carried out a study of wastage and stagnation in primary education in tribal areas. Major objectives of the study were to find out the nature and extent of wastage and stagnation and to identify the causes responsible for it. Sample of the study consisted of 104 schools from two tribal blocks of eight tribal districts of Gujarat. Questionnaires were administered and interviews were conducted on parents, teachers and educational inspectors for the collection of data. Findings of the study revealed that: (1) the rate of wastage in the first four years of schooling was found to 65 per cent; (2) The combined rates of wastage and stagnation in all the fifteen blocks were 83.6 per cent and 84.9 per cent respectively for the two different cohorts; (3) Wastages were greater amount girls than among boys in almost all the blocks.

Medhi, S. (1978) carried out an investigation into the probable causes of stagnation and wastage among the pupils of secondary schools of Kamrup district. The major objectives of the study were to find out the extent of stagnation and wastage and to find out the causes of these problems. The sample of the study included 100 head-masters, one inspector of schools 100 stagnated students and drop-outs and 40 guardians. The study revealed: (1) the extent of wastage and stagnation was very high especially in economically backward classes; (2) Other causal actors were illiteracy of the parents, their poverty, and lack of study, atmosphere at home and the rate and irregular payments of the stipend.

Raj N.K. (1979) conducted a study of the socio-economic factors and interrelation ships among the out-of-school children. The purposes of the study were to enumerate the out of school children in the age group 6-11 years and to find out the socio-economic factor that characterised the out of school children. The non-probability sampling procedure was used on the basis of which 54 drop-outs and 659 left-outs were included in the study. Results of the study indicated that: (*i*) there was a decreasing trend in percentage from lower to higher age categories for the left-outs whereas, the corresponding trend for the drop-outs was an increasing one; (*ii*) drop-outs were found more in larger families; (*iii*) the percentage of out of school children was higher in those families which were low in family literacy index; (*iv*) the percentage was higher in nuclear families than in joint families.

Pandey, B.B. (1979) investigated into adjustment problems of adolescents. The sample of the study was 500 students studying in class XI. The tests used were the Adjustment inventory and the test on the level of Aspiration. The findings of the investigation were: (*i*) rural students secured better points in emotional, health and adjustment areas; (*ii*) significant relationship existed between adjustment and achievement; (*iii*) urban students were facing difficulty in adjustment in school, heath and educational areas.

Das, R.C. (1979) conducted a study on effectiveness of Teacher Training in reducing educational wastage. The aim of the study was to find out the impact of teacher training on educational wastage and stagnation in primary schools. 743 schools from representative rural districts was the sample of the survey. Important findings of the study were: (*i*) training of teachers had no significant impact on the system of education at the primary school; (*ii*) the training of teachers at the primary level had no significant contribution towards reduction of wastage and stagnation in schools with multiple class teaching; (*iii*) the rate if stagnation in multiple teacher schools with a majority of trained teachers was 60.71 per cent against 56.50 per cent for schools with a majority of untrained teachers.

Aiskara, J. (1979) conducted a study of educating 'out of school' children. The purposes of the study were to have a preliminary idea about the magnitude of the 'out of school children' and five per cent random sample on the 'in-school' children were drawn for the purpose of interviewing parents/guardians. The major findings were: (1) the out of school children had a relatively poorer educational, occupational and economic background; (2) poverty and poor educational background stood out as the main reasons for drop-outs and failure to enter school; (3) by and large, parents of out of school, children were eager and willing to send their children to an educational programme that would be suitable and convenient to them.

Seetharamu, A.S. (1980) conducted a study of the utilisation for educational facilities by slum-dwellers of

Bangalore city in relation to their social and economic backgrounds. The main purpose of the study was to find out the participatory behaviour in schooling in slum areas and the utilisation facilities. A sample of 1000 children, 500 drop-outs and 500 stay-ins was selected by stratified random sampling. Important findings of the study were: (1) the total drop-out rates at the end of Standard I, II, III and IV were 46.20, 24.20, 19.00 and 9.60 per cent respectively; (2) mother in unskilled occupation contributed the highest percentage of drop-outs; (3) as many as 38.60 per cent of drop-outs did not work at home while remaining 61.40 did one work or the other.

Sarkar, B.N (1980) carried out a pilot investigation on school drop-out reasons. The main aim of the study was to ascertain the reasons for drop-out and prepare a list of reasons applicable to the rural population of the country. A questionnaire consisting of ninety-three questions was administered on a sample of forty-six male and thirty-five female drop-outs in the age group 6-14 years. Guardians of the drop-out were also interviewed. The investigation revealed that: (1) school environment did not contribute to the drop-out of students of either sex. Domestic work accounted for at least 70 per cent of female drop-outs; (2) inadequate income for living accounted for two third of the female drop-outs and about 80 per cent of the male drop-outs; (3) guardian's lack of interest was the most dominant reason applicable to both the male and female drop-outs.

Qureshi, A.N. (1980) conducted study of creativity in relation to (*i*) intelligence, manifest anxiety and level of aspiration are related to creativity; (*ii*) How much and in what way intelligence, anxiety and level of aspiration influenced creativity; (*iii*) The dynamics of aspiration statistical technique involving analysis of variance and coefficient of correlation were used. The sample was drawn from Firozabad town and there hundred girls of high school and intermediate classes were selected. Creativity test of Mehdi, Group of Aspiration Inventory (Patel). Findings of the study revealed that (*i*) TEST of Mental Ability (Jalota), STAT by Shema and Singh and level intelligence was significantly and positively related to intelligence (*ii*) anxiety appeared to be positively correlated to creativity; (*iii*) intelligence, anxiety and aspiration level promoted creativity and its components; (*iv*) aspiration level was related to creativity and its components.

Pillai, G.V., Benjamin, J. and Nair K.R., (1980) carried out a study of drop-outs in primary education in Kerala. The major objectives of the study were to identify the socio-economic causes leading to drop-outs. Sample consisted of twenty-eight lower schools selected from twenty-eight educational sub-districts with due representation to highland, middle and costal regions in the state. Four hundred seventy nine house lands were surveyed for the purpose. The major findings of the study were: (1) The percentage of drop-outs was higher among boys than among girls; (2) Students belonging to SC, ST and other backward communities constituted the majority of the drop-outs (69%); (3) the main reasons of drop-outs were ill health, household work, and poverty in that order; (4) a majority of drop-outs were children of casual labourers.

Vathsala, S. (1981) conducted study of initial drop-outs at Middle school level. The purposes of the study were: (*i*) to identify the causes for drop-out and to examine the inter relationship among the various factors related to drop-outs. Thirty drop-outs and thirty staying were selected as the sample of the study. Tools used for the study were the socio-economic scale (Pareek and Trivedi) school Adjustment Inventory (Saroji), Self Acceptance Scale (Kakkar), Junior Eysenck personality inventory and Achievement Motivation Inventory (Mehta). The Investigator also used semi-structured interview schedule, and schematic differential scale. The study revealed that: (1) Potential drop-outs hailed from poor, illiterate, wage earner families; (2) poor achievement in reading and number abilities and failure were associated with potential drop-outs; (3) drop-outs were neurotics, had low acceptance and achievements motivation; (4) as potential drop-outs, there was no significant difference between boys and girls; (5) potential drop-outs liked the schools.

Joshi, N.D. (1981) studied the problems faced by certain tribal groups in Trivanderum district. The purposes of the study were to find out the causes of the high drop-outs among tribal areas and to find out the causes of the high drop-outs among tribal students. Data were collected by interviewing 400 Kanikhar families and by administering a questionnaire to 54 teachers from eight schools. Results of the study indicated that: (1) school facilities within one kilometer were available to 18 per cent; (2) Tribal families felt that the teachers did not show favourable attitude towards the education of tribal children; (3) Poverty, lack of learning materials, language difficulty, lack of school facilities, in accessibility of schools, ignorance of parents, child labour and parents compulsion were among the factors responsible for their dropping out of schools and for their non-entrance.

A.N. Sinha (1981) carried out a survey of non-enrolled, non-attending and drop-out children of 6-14 age groups in Hazaribag District. Fifty schools belonging to fifty villages were sampled for the study. Data were collected through household schedules, school information bank and interview schedules. Major findings of the study were: (1) 60.31 per cent children were enrolled; 31.68 per cent children were non-enrolled and 8.091 per cent children were drop-outs in the age group 6-14; (2) The percentage of enrolment increased with increase in family income, however, the incidence of drop-outs was not related to income; (3) The drop-outs were significantly correlated with the number of teachers in the school.

Husain., M. (1982) Conducted an investigation of wastage and stagnation in primary schools of Bhilwara District. The aim of the study was to find out the wastage and stagnation as well as the teacher pupil ratio in urban and rural areas. Primary schools of all Panchayat Samitis of Builwara District were selected as the sample of the study. The narrative survey method was used for the study. Major findings were as follows: (1) The rate of wastage was higher in the first two classes; (2) Out of 682 primary schools, 506 were single teacher's schools and in these the rate of wastage was also higher; (3) The teacher pupil ratio in Rajasthan as a whole was 1: 49 whereas, in rural areas if Bhilwara District it was found to be 1: 26.

Mathur, J.S., Jain S.P. and Rahim, C.A. (1982) carried out an investigation on rural youths from poverty groups: Drop-outs and non-students. The investigation was based on the following objectives:

(*i*) To examine the SES of school / college drop-outs and non-student youths;

(*ii*) To identify causal factors for their withdrawal.

Sample of the study was 1900 respondents selected through multi-staged randomised process. Important findings were: (*i*) most of the parents felt that school timings were unsuitable and did not provide adequate opportunity to the children to be helpful in their family education; (*ii*) The reasons mentioned by non-students for not attending school were poor financial position, parental ignorance, need to supplement family income, frequent migration of parents, unforeseen eventualities such as sickness etc.; (*iii*) in case of drop-outs, parental ignorance, involvement in work, lack of interest in studies and failure in examination were the reasons.

Khanna, K. (1983) conducted an investigation on preparation of reading material for girl drop-outs in Delhi slums. Objectives of the study were: (*i*) to develop need based and interesting reading material for girl drop-outs; (*ii*) to test the effectiveness of the reading material developed for the study Interview schedule. Ability test, Achievement test and questionnaire were the tools conducted on a sample of 103 girls. Major findings were found to be: (*i*) respondents by and large, belonged to nuclear families of seven members on an average and Rs. 3000/- as an annual income; (*ii*) the most common reason was found to be parent's education was almost negligible; (*iii*) the value of R between the three components of reading ability and cumulative learning was 0.71 which was substantial and significant; (*iv*) After exposure to the module, the average score of the girl drop-outs on the questionnaire increased from 7.5 to 13.5 indicating a positive shift.

Devi, K.G. (1983) finds out the problems of drop-outs in primary schools of Manipur with special reference to Imphal town. The investigation aimed at to ascertain accurately the extent and nature of drop-out problem and to study various situations. The careers of 54497 and 2927 fresh entrants in class 'A' in 1961 had been followed upto class VII in 1969 in Manipur and Imphal town respectively as the study. The major findings of the study revealed that: (*i*) the difference in rate between boys and girls was 14.26 per cent; (*ii*) the difference between the mean rate of drop-out boys and girls was 6.30; (*iii*) the highest rate of drop-out appeared in class A (48.48 per cent) and lowest in class VI (4.79%); (*iv*) Poverty, frequent transfer, repeated failures and negligence of parents were the main causes of drop-outs.

Dass, J.R., and Garg, V.P. (1985) studied in impact of preprimary education on drop-outs, stagnation and academic performance. The study was carried out in 18 schools of Delhi Municipal Corporation. For the study of drop-outs, the total numbers of students covered were 10.082 from schools with nursery sections. A sample of 789 class V students was taken to see the effect of pre-school education on educational achievement. Results of the study indicated that (*i*) early childhood education had a salutary effect in case of the group which was pre-school education; (*iii*) slightly higher achievement was also observed in class V among students who attended pre-primary education.

Rather A.R. (1985) carried out a study on incidence of drop-outs and maladjustments among students in relation to creativity and social structure of the school. Main objectives of the study were: (*i*) to study the relationship between incidence of drop-outs and socio-metric status of pupils; (*ii*) to study the relationship between incidence of drop-out and creativity; (*iii*) to study the relationship between Adjustment of pupils and their creativity; (*iv*) to study the relationship between SES, incidence of drop-outs and Adjustments. Sample of the study comprised 887 students ranging age from 11-14 years. Stratified techniques applied were t-test, Chi-square test and product moment correlation. Main findings of the study were: (*i*) the incidence of drop-outs was positively related with socio-metric status of the child in the class room; (*ii*) the drop-out incidence was significantly related to SES of children; (*iii*) the relationship between Adjustment and SMS was found to be significant and positive. The same was the case between Adjustment and Creativity; (*v*) Creativity and Adjustment were not significantly related.

S. Subramanyam (1986), studied the problem of school drop-outs with special reference to scheduled castes and scheduled tribes. The main purpose of the study was to identify the relative influence of personal, economic and socio-cultural problem of school drop-outs. A sample of 300 drop-outs in 30 areas covering three districts of Andhra Pradesh was selected by stratified random sampling procedure. Problem checklist was developed to enumerate the problems of drop-outs. The findings of the study revealed that; (*i*) the problem in the area of personal factors such as Adjustment to the present educational set up are considerably high and this situation is very severe in the case of girls and with regard to children belonging to scheduled tribes; (*ii*) the economic problem of school drop-outs are also considerable high in the case of SC's and

ST's; (*iii*) the social problems are also considerably high in case of scheduled tribes; (*iv*) there was no significant difference in the sub areas of economic and social problems and boys are more suffered in the area of personal problems.

SIE, U.P., (1986) conducted a study of drop-outs and failures in primary classes. The main purpose of the study was to study the causes of drop-outs and failures among 6-14 age group students. The study was delimited to the four regions of the state, namely the middle zone, eastern zone, southern zone and western zone. The findings revealed that: (*i*) in all the four developed blocks, the development trend showed that from 6-8 class, 15 per cent were drop-outs and four per cent were failures; (*ii*) maximum drop-outs were seen among children coming from backward classes; (*iii*) the main causes for drop-outs were illiteracy of the parents, poverty, lack of interest distance of school from home, unattractive environment of the school, indifference of teachers, irrelevant curriculum, lack of physical facilities like water and sanitation etc., in schools.

Dianes, Kaplin, B.Mitchell Peck, Howard B. Kaplan (1990) conducted a study—Decomposing the academic failure, drop-out relationship: A longitudinal analysis. Data from a four—wave panel (N = 195) tested in the 7th, 8th and 9th grades and as young adults, were used to estimate a causal model. The model was used to decompose a previously, observed term of 5 theoretically informed mediating variables. The academic failure drop-outs relationship was partially decomposed by mediating effect of low motivation, association with deviant peers and perception of rejection by the students at school. Although perception of rejection by teachers and resistance towards school were, as hypothesized, influenced by earlier negative academic experience. They had no independent effect on dropping out not of their relationship to associate with deviant peers or low motivation. Implications for current practices and future research are also discussed.

Stevenson, R.B. and Ellsworth, J. (1991) conducted a study on dropping out in a working class high schools, adolescent voices on the decision to leave. Finding reveals how the schools response, or lack thereof, to student's problem compound their difficulties and create tensions over the source of blame for their failure. However, these adolescents also attributed much of their failure of themselves. In revealing the issue of blame, these suburban white drop-outs in contrast to immercify minority youth believed that they must be at fault for failing to conform to the expectation and demands of schools.

Mc.Caul, Edward, et al (1992) Studied the consequences of dropping out of school, findings from high school and beyond. The purpose of the present study was to examine the personal, social and economic consequences of dropping out of school. Drop-out differed from graduates with no post secondary education on many personal and social adjustments measures. Results indicated that male and female drop-outs have different personal, social and economic experience.

Flisher, A.J. and Chalton, D.O. (1995) conducted a study in high school drop-outs in a working class South African community, selected characteristics and risk-taking behaviour. Structured questionnaire data from household heads and adolescent drop-outs in a working class South African community were used to explore drop-outs. Characteristics and the prevalence of their risk taking behaviour compared with those attending school of the 548 teenagers sampled 15.9 per cent were drop-outs, of these 62.1 per cent left school after less than years. Those still attending to school were more likely to engage in suicidal behaviour, but less likely to abuse substances and (for girls) to have had sexual intercourse.

Jordon, will J., Lara and McPartland, James (1996), explored the causes of early drop-out among race—ethnic and gender groups. This study used nationally representative high school student data to show race—ethnicity and gender difference in reasons for early school drop-outs and plans for drop-outs to resume their education. Factor analysis shows that separate reasons for dropping out include school related, family related and job related causes as well as influences from peers and residential mobility. White drop-outs cited alienation from school, more often than their African-Americans or Hispanic of both sexes. African American males reported being responded or expelled from school more than the other groups. Hispanic and African American females cited family reasons more often than did white females.

Teachman Joy D., Paasch and Carver Karen (1996) conducted the study of social capital and dropping out of school early. A large sample of data was taken from the national educational longitudinal survey to examine the effects of various measures of social capital on the likelihood of dropping out of school early, before 10th grade controlling for indicators of the financial and human capitals of parents. Result indicated that more specific indicators of social capital (patterns of parental interaction, number of times the child changed school) can account for all the effect of attending a catholic school, but only a fraction of the effect of family structure on leaving school early.

Chapter 3

Profile of the Study Area

DISTRICT PROFILE

Perambalur district is a centrally located inland district of Tamil Nadu, spread over 3690.07 sq.kms, which was trifurcated from the erstwhile composite Tiruchirappalli district and was formed on 1 November 1995. The district is bounded by Cuddalore district in the north, Tiruchirappalli district in the South, Thanjavur in the East and Namakkal and Tiruchirappalli districts in the West.

The total Geographical area of the district is 369007 ha. and net sown area and gross sown area are 216422 ha. and 237136 ha. respectively. The net area under irrigation is 71624 ha. The total population of the district as per 2001 census is 11,81,029 of which 5,88,441 are males and 5,92,588 are females. The sex ratio is 1007 with the birth rate at 21.6 and the death rate at 7.7. The density of population of the district per sq. k.m. is 281 persons as against the stage average of 429 persons.

The district for administrative purpose has been divided into six Taluks (Perambalur, Kunnam, Veppanthattai, Ariyalur, Sendurai and Jayakondam) which is further sub-divided into ten blocks *viz.,* (Perambalur, Veppanthattai,

Veppur, Alathur, Ariyalur, Thirumanur, Sendurai, Jayakondam, Andimadam and T.Palur) comprising of 345 villages, 322 village Panchayats and Nine Panchayats.

The district lies in the Southern plateau and hill zone of Agro-climate regional planning with characteristics of semi arid climate. The soil is predominantly red loamy and black soil. The normal rainfall of the district is 908 mm, which is less than 946.9 mm, the normal rainfall of the State. The precipitation during northeast monsoon, southwest monsoon and remaining winter and hot weather period account for 52 per cent, 34 per cent and 14 per cent of annual rainfall respectively.

Cauvery is the major river flowing in the region and the composite district has a canal system. Covering just 47 kms stretch and ayacut of 11610 ha. The ground water resource through tube wells and wells contribute nearly 68 per cent of irrigated area command. The major crops grown in the district are paddy, groundnut, sugarcane and millets. Cashew is the major plantation crop.

There are a total of 47 PHCs in the district of which 37 are additional PHCs, 7 are block and 3 are 24 hour PHCs. The number of primary schools, middle schools, high schools and higher secondary schools are 722, 118, 82 and 67 respectively.

ADMINISTRATIVE UNITS

Revenue Division	
1.	Perambalur
2.	Ariyalur
3.	Udaiyarpalayam

Taluk

Sl. No.	Taluk Name
1.	Perambalur
2.	Veppanthattai

3.	Kunnam
4.	Ariyalur
5.	Sendurai
6.	Udaiyarpalayam

Block

Sl. No.	Block Name
1.	Perambalur
2.	Veppanthattai
3.	Veppur
4.	Alathur
5.	Ariyalur
6.	Thirmanur
7.	Sendurai
8.	T. Palur
9.	Andimadam
10.	Jayankondam

REVENUE VILLAGE

Sl. No.	Revenue Village
1.	Esanni
2.	Alangali
3.	Keelakkarai
4.	Elambalur
5.	Sangonam
6.	Thoramangalam
7.	Perambalur (South)
8.	Perambalur (North)
9.	Aranarai (South)
10.	Aranarai (North)
11.	Kurumbalur (South)
12.	Kurumbalur (North)

13.	Melapuliyur (East)
14.	Melapuliyur (West)
15.	Ladapuram (West)
16.	Ladapuram (East)
17.	Ammapalayam
18.	Kalarampatti
19.	Chatramani
20.	Bommanappadi
21.	Velur
22.	Pudunaduvalur
23.	Siruvacher
24.	Nochiyam
25.	Kalpadi (North)
26.	Kalpadi (South)
27.	Ayilur

Panchayat Villagers

Sl.No.	Panchayat Village
1.	Ammapalayam
2.	Ayilur
3.	Alambadi
4.	Bommanappadi
5.	Chattramani
6.	Esanni
7.	Elambalur
8.	Kalpadi
9.	Kalarampatti
10.	Kavulpalayam
11.	Koneripalayam
12.	Kilakarai
13.	Ladapuram

14.	Melapuliyur
15.	Nochiyam
16.	Pudunaduvalur
17.	Siruvachur
18.	Sangonam
19.	Vadakkumadevi
20.	Velur

Particulars	Perambalur District		
	Male	Female	Total
Total Population	588441	592588	1181029

Panchayats

Sl. No	Details of Wards	Total
1.	Hamlets	924
2.	Panchayats	322
3.	Panchayat Wards	1107
4.	Panchayat Unions	10
5.	Panchayat Union Wards	189
6.	District Panchayat Wards	8/12

Street Lights

Sl. No	Details of Wards	Total
1.	Tube Lights	27030
2.	Sodium Vapours	2891
3.	Others	453
	Total	**30374**

Agriculture Department

The agriculture department in the district is headed by Joint Director of Agriculture. As the district is mainly agrarian, the improvement of productivity, production and profitability becomes most important objective of the department in the district. Secondly the agro climatic zone of the district is favourable for cultivation of some of the medicinal and aromatic plants. The district has the largest area under cotton cultivation.

EDUCATION—DISTRICT PRIMARY EDUCATION PROGRAMME

Introduction

District Primary Education Programme has been launched in this district since November 1997. The main criteria for selecting this District are the lower level of the female literacy rate than the national literacy at the time of introduction of District Primary Education Programme.

Aims and Objectives of DPEP

1. Enrolment of all the school age children in the age group of 6 to 11.
2. Retention of all the enrolled children in schools without any dropout.
3. Completing five year of Primary Education with quality.
4. Promoting of Girls Education.
5. Provision of Integrated Education for the Disabled children.
6. Involving the community for the better functioning of schools.

Schemes of DPEP

Buildings were taken up for construction both by the Public Works Department and the community participation work. 69 schools were benefited under the scheme.

Alternative Schools

In order to provide inclusive education for the drop-out and non-enrolled children including migrated and child labour children. Alternative schools have been started in all blocks.

1. Perambalur	6 Centres
2. Alathur	3 Centres
Beneficiaries	**180 Children**

SC/ST Special Coaching Classes

To promote girls education, particularly children belongs to SC/ST community, Special Coaching classes were started for the above girl children in 3, 4 and 5 standards. Being the first generation learners, the SC/ST children could not complete the children of the other social groups. But now from February 2002 onwards, SC/ST boy's children have also been included under the above scheme. Disabled children have also been included along with SC/ST children.

Beneficiaries

Total No. of Schools	172
Total No. Centres	342
Beneficiaries SC/ST	**9555 (4919 + 4636)**
Beneficiaries IED	484 (299 + 185)
Total Beneficiaries	**9939 (5218+4821)**

Training Programmes

Quality improvement is one of the major objectives of DPEP. Many of the schools have multi-grade teaching situation *i.e.,* single teacher has to handle more than one classes. The teachers are given following types of training to improve their teacher skills in such situations.

- To teach more than one subjects.
- Refresher cum Booster course.
- English training to teacher handling 3, 4 and 5 standards.
- Training an Activity-based joyful teaching methodology.
- Training to newly appointed teachers.
- Training to teachers who handled SC/ST special coaching classes.
- Preparation of Teaching Learning Material.

Teaching Learning Material and Infrastructure Grant

All the teacher working in Primary classess are provided with the above grant at Rs. 500/- every year for purchasing teaching material Rs. 2000/- per year sanctioned to all schools to improve the infrastructure facilities.

Early Childhood Education

The ECE centres facilitate the girl child to attend schools by relieving them from the sibling care responsibilities. Being the feeder institution of Primary Schools, the Child Welfare Organisers are given two days training programme every year. Apart from that, the DPEP has also programmed to supply teacher and learning materials at Rs. 1000/- per centre.

Integrated Education for the Disabled Children

Universalisation of Primary Education cannot be prescribed unless we mainstream all the disabled children. 9 Special teachers as various impairments are working to cater to the needs of the 384 disabled children. One medical camp was conducted at Perambalur Block. Similar camps are programmed in the remaining blocks. Aids and appliances have also been supplied with the help of Rehabilitation Department.

Jeyankondam Block

In Jeyankondam block according to the census report, it has a population of 31,268 in total of which 41 per cent are male and 59 per cent are female. 11 per cent of the total population is below 60 years of age. The total literacy of the block is 69 per cent. Out of the 11,612/- of the job holders 8,042 are male and 3,210 are female. The block has 35 villages and 21 schools, out of which 14 are primary, 3 are high school and the remaining 4 are higher secondary schools.

Research Methodology

Chapter 4

INTRODUCTION

The present chapter deals with the methodology of the study. First section deals with design of the study. The second section deals with the objectives of the study. The hypotheses are presented in section three. The fourth section describes the selection sample. The fifth section explains the tool used. The sixth section deals with data analysis with statistical technique used. The seventh section covers the limitations of the study.

Table 4.1

S.No.	Type	Source
1.	Nature of the Research	Normative Survey
2.	Variables	I. Academic factors II. Economic factors III. Social factors
3.	Tool Used	Attitude towards academic, economic and social factors
4.	Sampling Technique	Stratified Random Sampling
5.	Size of Sample	100 drop-outs of Jeyankondam Block

DESIGN OF THE STUDY

Research design is facilitating the smooth sailing of the various research operations, thereby making research as efficient as possible yielding maximum information with minimum expenditure of effort, time and money.

Kerlinger (1973), as pointed out that research investigation conceived so as to obtain to control variance.

Sub Sample

		Primary		Upper Primary	
I.	Sex	Male	: 23	Male	: 26
		Female	: 24	Female	: 27
II.	Community	SC	: 21	SC	: 26
		MBC	: 18	MBC	: 20
		BC	: 8	BC	: 7
III.	Willing and non-willing to go to school	Willing	: 23	Willing	: 29
		Non-willing	: 24	Non-willing	: 24
IV.	Nature of the work of the drop-outs	Daily Wages	: 26	Daily Wages	: 28
		Vendors	: 21	Vendors	: 25

Statistical Technique used—Mean, Standard Deviation and 't' test

As shown in the above table, the nature of the study is normative survey. The variables in the study were Academic, Economic, and Social Factors, As the standardised tool was not available, the investigator himself developed a tool, named "Academic, Economic and social factors influencing drop-out children. The tool used was 5 point scale to measures the attitude of drop-out children. The investigator used the stratified random sample technique in the study. The size of the sample was 100 which were selected systematically out of the total sample 400 in Jeyankondam Block. The total sample was sub-divided with respect to sex, community, willing and unwilling to go to school and nature of the dropouts. The collected data was analysed with the use of different statistical techniques.

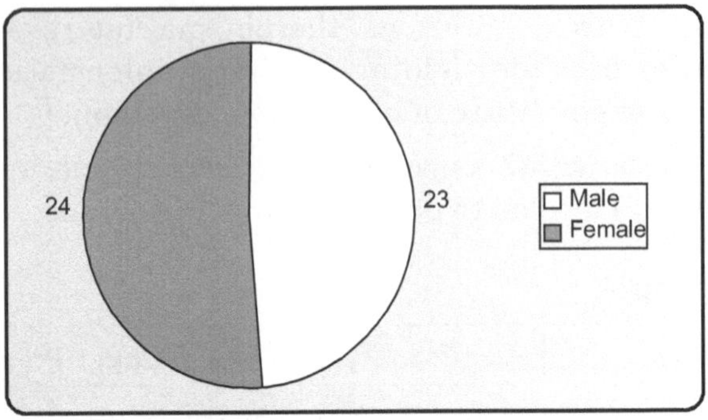

Chart—4.1. Pie Diagram showing different sub-samples of the Primary Level – Sex

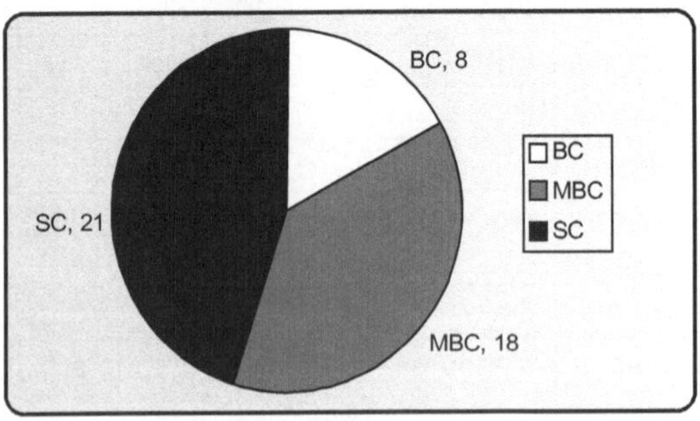

Chart—4.2. Pie Diagram showing different sub-samples of the Primary Level Study—Community

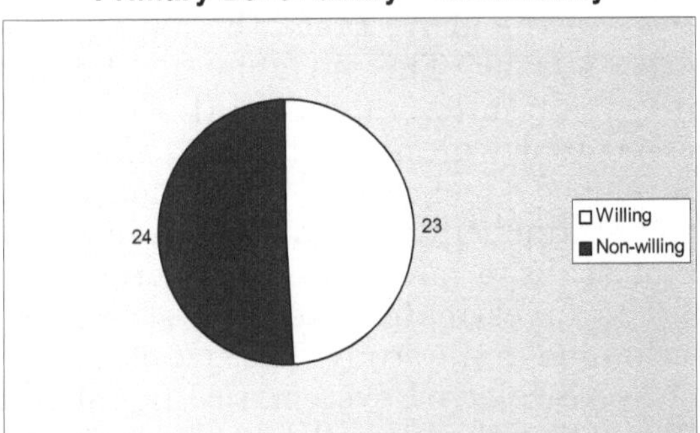

Chart—4.3. Pie Diagram showing different sub-samples of the study—Willing and Non-willing to go to school at Primary Level

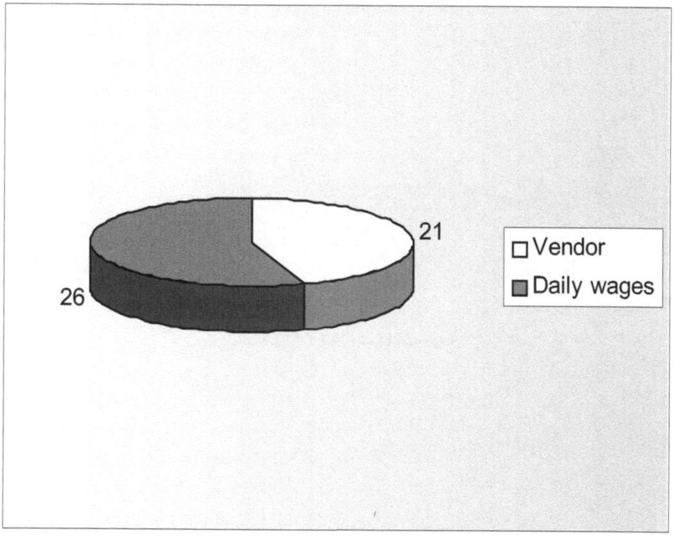

Chart—4.4. Pie Diagram showing different sub-samples of the study-Nature of Work of the Drop-outs at Primary Level

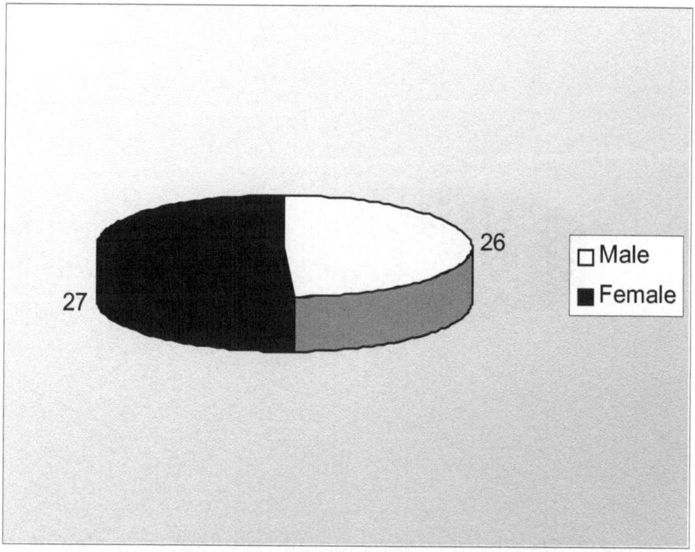

Chart—4.5. Pie Diagram showing different sub-samples of the study—Sex at Upper Primary Level

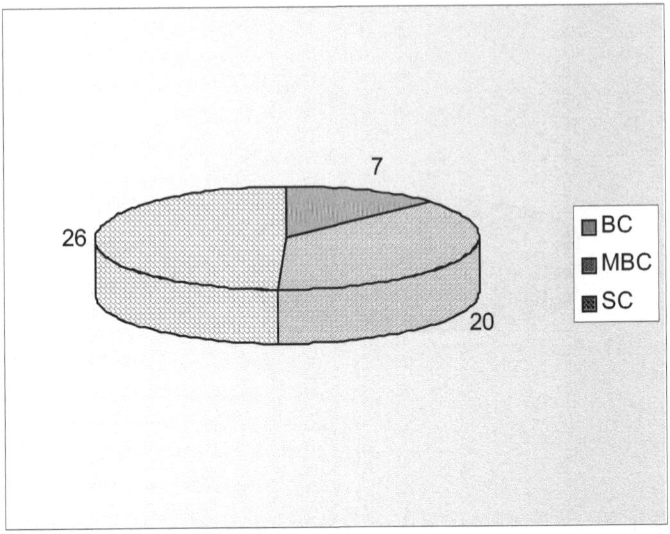

Chart—4.6. Pie Diagram showing different sub-samples of the study—Community at Upper Primary Level

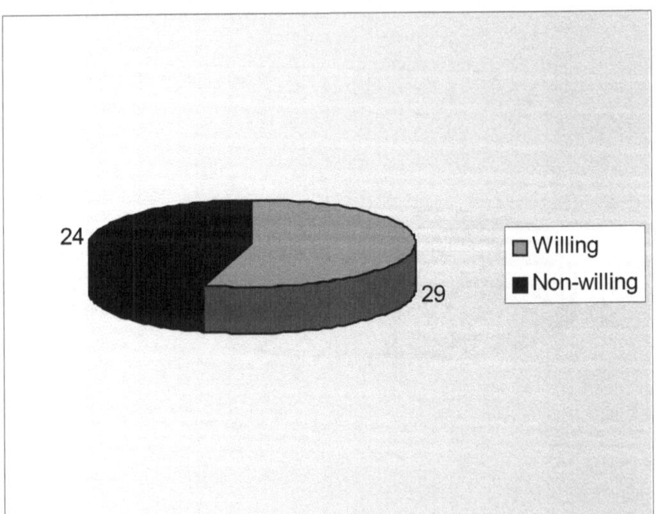

Chart—4.7. Pie Diagram showing different sub-samples of the study—Willing and Non-willing to go to school at Upper Primary Level

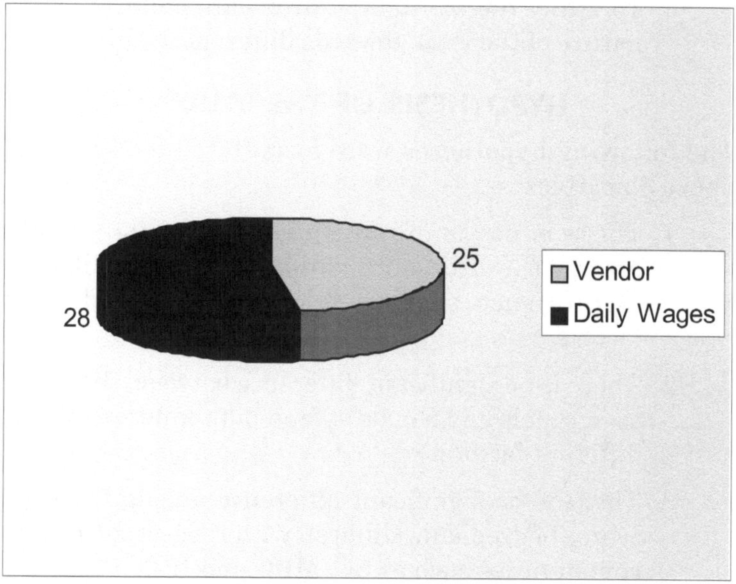

Chart—4.8. Pie Diagram showing different sub-samples of the study—Nature of to work of the drop-outs at Upper Primary Level.

OBJECTIVES OF THE STUDY

The main objectives of the study is the Attitude of dropout children among primary and upper primary level in Jeankondam Block towards different factors such as academic, economic and social factors. The specific objectives are as follows:

1. To study the attitude of male and female drop-outs children towards different factors;
2. To study the attitude of drop-outs children belonging to different communities. SC, MBC, and BC towards different factors;
3. To study the attitude to drop-outs children whose willing and non-willing to go to school towards different factors.

4. To study the attitude of drop-outs children whose nature of the work towards different factors.

HYPOTHESIS OF THE STUDY

The following hypotheses were formulated to realise the above objectives:

1. There is no significant difference on the attitude among the drop-outs children towards different factors such as academic, economic and social factors.
2. There is no significant difference between the means scores male and female of drop-outs children towards different factors.
3. There is no significant difference among the mean scores of drop-outs children with respect to different communities such as SC, MBC and BC.
4. There is no significant difference among the means scores of drop-outs children whose willing and unwilling to go to school.
5. There is no significant difference the mean scores of drop-outs children whose nature of the work towards different factors.

SAMPLE SIZE

The primary and upper primary drop-outs children in Jeyankondam Block were the population of the study. They are 400 drop-outs children among primary and upper primary level in Jeyankondam Union. Based on the stratified random sampling techniques, the investigator selected 100 samples. The students of standard 9 and 10 were not included in the study. The drop-outs children whose were studying from 1-5th and 6-8th standard were included in the study. The names of the cluster resources centre of Jeyankondam Block Resource Centre and Strength of the students are given below.

Table 4.2 Name and Strength of the sample

S. No.	Name and Place of the CRC	Strength
1.	Jeyankondam	10
2.	Meensuruty	10
3.	Udayarpalayam	10
4.	Kangaikondasolapuram	10
5.	Mangathi	10
6.	Pakalamedu	10
7.	B.P. Nallur	10
8.	Sarvamadam	10
9.	Old Jeyankondam	10
10.	Erumbulikurichi	10
	Total	**100**

The total sample was sub-divided with respect to sex, community, willing and unwilling to go to school, nature of work of the drop-outs children.

The size of the sample with respect to sex are presented in the following chart 4.9.

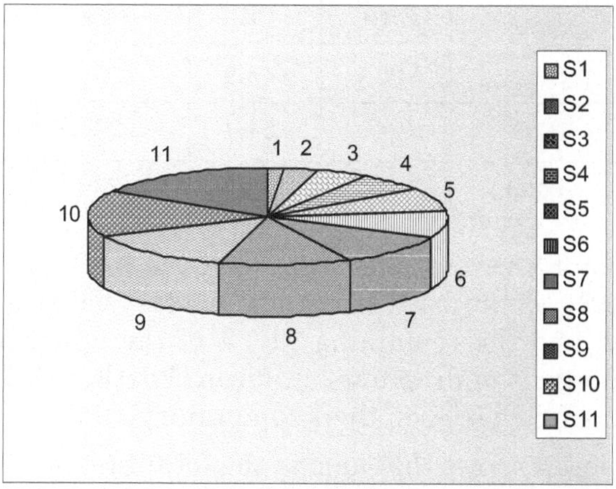

Chart—4.9. Pie Diagram showing the different strengths of the Sample—Primary Level

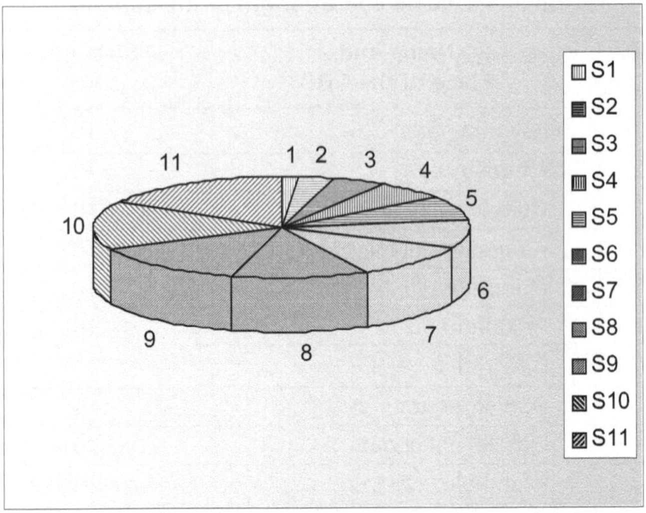

Chart—4.10. Pie Diagram showing the different strengths of the Study—Upper Primary Level

Table 4.3. Sample based on Sex in Primary and Upper Primary Level

S.No.	Category	Primary Level		Upper Primary Level	
		Size	%	Size	%
1.	Boys	23	48.9	26	49.0
2.	Girls	24	51.1	27	51.0
	Total	**47**	**100.0**	**53**	**100.0**

Table 4.3 reveals that 48.9% of the boys in primary level, 49% of the boys in upper primary level dropouts children and the remaining 51.1% of the upper primary level and girls of drop-outs children. Further the sample was classified based on their community.

Table 4.4 shows that among the total sample 47, 47.7% are scheduled caste, 38.2% are most backward community and sample 17.1% are backward caste in Primary level.

Table 4.4 Sample based on Community in Primary and Upper Primary Level

S.No.	Category	Primary Level		Upper Primary Level	
		Size	%	Size	%
1.	Schedule Caste (SC)	21	44.7	26	49.0
2.	Most Backward Class (MBC)	18	38.2	20	37.7
3.	Backward Class (BC)	8	17.1	7	13.3
	Total	**47**	**100.0**	**53**	**100.0**

In the upper primary level the total sample was 53, 49% are scheduled caste, sample 37.7% are most backward community and sample 13.3% are backward caste. Further the sample was classified based on the willing and non willing to go to school in primary and upper primary level.

Table 4.5. Sample based on Willing and Non-willing to go to school in Primary and Upper Primary Level

S.No.	Category	Primary Level		Upper Primary Level	
		Size	%	Size	%
1.	Willing to go to school	23	48.9	29	54.7
2.	Non-willing to go to school	24	51.1	24	45.3
	Total	**47**	**100.0**	**53**	**100.0**

Table 4.5 shows that among the total sample 47, 48.9% are willing to go to school, sample 51.1% are non-willing to go to school in Primary level.

In the upper primary level, the total sample was 53, 54.7% are willing to go to school, sample 45.3% are non-willing to go to school.

For further analysis the sample was classified based on their nature of the work of the drop-outs children in primary and upper primary level.

Table 4.6. Sample based on nature of the work of dropouts children in Primary and Upper Primary Level

S.No.	Category	Primary Level		Upper Primary Level	
		Size	%	Size	%
1.	Daily wages	26	55.3	28	52.8
2.	Vendors	21	44.7	25	47.2
	Total	**47**	**100.0**	**53**	**100.0**

Table 4.6 shows that among the total sample 47, 55.3% of daily wages and sample 44.7% of vendors in Primary level.

TOOL USED IN THE STUDY

The investigator himself developed the 5 point attitude scale.

Preparation of Preliminary Draft of Academic, Economic and Social Factors

As the investigator was much interested on the education of drop-outs children throughout at Jeyankondam block in Perambalur District, he went on coining suitable items to measures the attitudes towards different factors such as Academic, Economic and Social factors.

The investigator selected both positive and negative items. To elicit the reliable response from the subjects strongly agree of positive items gets 5 and agree, undesired, disagree and strongly disagree gets 4, 3, 2 and 1 respectively. Likewise, "The negatively items gets 5 strongly agree gets 1 and agree, undesired, disagree and strongly disagree gets 2, 3, 4 and 5 respectively. Accordingly all the statements were prepared. The investigator took care to prepare 5 points scale which deal with significant ideas. Certain item eliciting the same response and repletion of the words in the options were avoided.

Attention was given to have the items uniformly selected from different variables. After perusal of the items, certain items were deleted and certain items were added wherever necessary. After the investigator himself satisfied on the items prepared, it was given to the experts who are interested in this field, their suitable suggestions were carried out. After carrying out all these were 100 items in all three factors such as Academic, Economic and Social factors.

A blue print was prepared to check the items which are presented the following table given below.

Table 4.8. Blue Print for Preliminary drafts of Academic, Economic and Social Factors

S.No.	Factors	Item Numbers	Total	Percentage (%)
1.	Academic	1-36	36	36.0
2.	Economic	37-66	30	30.0
3.	Social	67-100	34	34.0
	Total		**100**	**100.0**

Item Analysis

The Investigator gave the statement of the questionnaire to the drop-outs children from Brammadiram in Marakkanam union. Based on the procedures of item analysis, all the items in the questionnaire were processed. On the basis of the results, the investigator changed some of the items and some of the items were modified.

Ultimately the total numbers of items were 72 out of 100 for the final study. The item selected for the final study are presented in the table 4.9.

Table 4.9 Blue Print for the find drafts of Academic, Economic and Social Factors

S.No.	Factors	Item Numbers	Total	Percentage (%)
1.	Academic	1-26	26	36.1
2.	Economic	27-46	20	27.8
3.	Social	47-72	26	36.1
	Total		**72**	**100**

The table 4.9 shows that the total item selected for the final study were 72 of which items related to factors of Academic are 36.1% Economic 27.8% Social 36.1%. Thus the tool was constructed by the investigator for the study.

Validity and Reliability

The investigator gave the questionnaire to the two teacher educators to verify the suitability of the items. Based on their suggestion medications was made. Thus the validity of tool was established. The investigator randomly selected 15 drop-outs children from Keelsiviri in Jeyankondam Union in Perambalur District. The prepared questionnaire was administered to them. After 15 days, the same questionnaire was administered to the same subjects the investigator valued the both questionnaire and found correlation co-efficient between the sets of the scores. The value of co-efficient of the reliability test was 0.87. Based on the result the tool was considered as highly valuable.

COLLECTION OF DATA

The tool was administered to 100 samples. The selection of samples for the final study was discussed under the sample selection. The Investigator asked the subjects to go through all their free time and put the tick mark in the attitude scale under the appropriate place in the questionnaire. The subjects were also instructed to note the positive and negative statements in the tool. After collecting the filled in a questionnaire the investigator second systematically. Thus the data required for the study were collected.

STATISTICAL TECHNIQUE

The collected data was systematically organised and suitable statistical techniques were applied to draw the precise solution in the study. Mean and standard deviation were calculated to find out t' value is in order to find out the significant difference between the two variables. Percentage was also used to analysis to data in the study.

LIMITATION OF THE STUDY

The limitations of the study are listed below:

1. The investigator found very limited research work in the area of drop-outs children in journals and survey of research.
2. The investigator confined his study with 100 samples, as it was difficult to identify them.

The forthcoming chapter deals with data analysis.

Analysis of Data

Chapter 5

OVERVIEW

Present chapter gives the details, about the analysis of the collected data. All the data were analysed with the level of significance of 0.05 level. Percentage, t-test, Chi-square test were the statistical techniques employed in the analysis of the data to draw meaningful generalisation. The data has been organised in four sections as follows:

CLASSIFICATION OF ANALYSIS

The data analysis has been organised in four sections as follows:

Section A This section deals with the analysis on the mean values of the different factors at primary and upper primary level.

Section B This section contains the analysis an factor-wise analysis at primary and upper primary level.

Section C This section reveals the analysis on the Academic factors with respect to demographic variables at primary and upper primary level.

Section D This section deals with the analysis on Economic factors with respect to demographic variables at primary and upper primary level.

Section E This section contains the analysis of Social factors with respect to demographic variables at primary and upper primary level.

SECTION-A

Mean Values of Different Factors at Primary an Upper Primary Level

From the collected data, mean values of different factors such as Academic, Economic and Social variables with respect to sex, community, willingness to go to school and present job responsible for drop-outs at Primary and Upper Primary levels was calculated. The results were presented in Table 5.1 and 5.2.

Table 5.1. Mean value of different factors responsible for drop-outs in Primary Level

S. No.	Category	Number of Children	Academic factor (%)	Economic Factor (%)	Social Factor (%)	Total
1.	Male	23	80.8	67.7	56.8	68.5
	Female	24	81.6	67	58.5	68.7
2.	SC & ST	21	81.4	67.1	59	69.3
	MBC & BC	26	81.2	67.4	58.2	69.1
3.	Willing to go to school	23	81.5	66.8	57.9	68.9
	Non-willing to go to school	24	81.1	67.7	58	69
4.	Daily wages	26	81.6	66.9	58.1	69
	Vendors	21	80.7	68.3	57.8	69

Form table 5.1, mean values obtained in three different factors represents that the mean value of Academic factor fall in the range between 80 and 82, Economic factor fall in the range between 66 and 69 and social factor fall in the range between 55 and 59 in the primary level.

At the same time the table's mean values fall in the range between 68 and 70. It is understood from this that the Academic factor stood first then Economic and Social factors responsible for the drop-outs of children at primary level.

Table 5.2 Mean value of different factors responsible for drop-outs in Upper Primary Level

S. No.	Category	Number of Children	Academic factor (%)	Economic Factor (%)	Social Factor (%)	Total
1.	Male	26	80.8	70	51.5	67.2
	Female	27	81	69.7	55.4	68.6
2.	SC & ST	26	93.5	71.9	56.1	70.4
	MBC & BC	27	80.3	70.3	54.9	68.5
3.	Willing to go to school	29	81	69.8	54.6	68.8
	Non-willing to go to school	24	80.8	69.8	54.8	68.4
4.	Daily wages	28	80.9	69.8	55.2	68.5
	Vendors	25	81	70.5	52.2	67.7

Form table 5.2, mean values obtained in three different factors represents that the mean value of Academic factor fall in the range between 80 and 81, Economic factor fall in the range between 68 and 71 and social factor fall in the range between 51 and 57. At the same time, the table's mean values fell in the range between 66 and 70.

It is understood from this that the Academic factor stood first when Economic and Social factors responsible for the drop-outs of children at primary level.

SECTION—B

Factor-wise Analysis at Primary and Upper Primary Level

This section deals with the analysis of data on the influence of Academic, Economic and Social Factors and its significance difference between them at primary and upper primary level.

Table 5.3. Significance of difference among the Academic, Economic and Social factors responsible for drop-outs students at Primary Level

S. No.	Category	N	M	SD	T	Remarks
1.	Academic	47	105.68	2.498	97.02	SD
	Economic	47	67.26	1.062		
2.	Academic	47	105.68	2.498	60.95	SD
	Social	47	75.23	2.243		
3.	Economic	47	67.26	1.062	22.02	SD
	Social	47	75.23	2.243		

Form the table 5.3, obtained that, 't' score value of 97.02, 60.95 and 22.02 with df 46 are greater than the table value 1.98 and are significant at 0.05 level. Hence, it is concluded that there was a significance of difference between the influence of the Academic and Economic Factors, Academic and Social factors and Economic and Social factors at primary level.

From the observed mean values, it shows that means values of Academic factors is more influencing for drop-outs than Social and Economic factors primary level. While comparing social and economic factors, social factors is significantly influencing for drop-outs than Economic factors at primary level.

Table 5.4. Significance of difference among the Academic, Economic and Social factors responsible for dropouts students at Upper Primary Level

S. No.	Category	N	M	SD	T	Remarks
1.	Academic	53	105.17	0.606	299.49	SD
	Economic	53	69.83	0.606		
2.	Academic	53	105.17	0.606	18.7	SD
	Social	53	69.92	13.71		
3.	Economic	53	69.93	0.606	0.048	SD
	Social	53	69.92	13.71		

Form the above table it was obtained 't' score value of 2999.49 and 18.7 respected by Academic, Economic and Academic, Social factors with df 46 are greater than 1.98 and are significant of 0.05 level

Hence, it is revealed that there was significance between the influence of the Academic and Economic Factors, Academic and Social factors at Upper Primary level.

From the observed mean values, it shows that means values of Academic factors is more influencing for drop-outs than social and Economic factors at Upper Primary level. While comparing Social factors Ps approximately equal to Economic factors at Upper primary level.

SECTION C

Analysis of Academic Factors with Respect to Demographic Variables

This section deals with the significance of difference of the mean values of Academic factors responsible for drop-outs with respect to gender that is male and female, community, willing and non-wiling to go to school and nature of work of the students at primary level and upper primary level.

Table 5.5. Significance of difference of mean values of Academic factors responsible for drop-outs with respect to gender at Primary Level

S. No.	Category	N	M	SD	T	Remarks
1.	Male	23	105.06	3.678	1.052	NSD
2.	Female	24	106.03	1.329		

Form the above table 5.5, it was obtained 't' Value 1.052 is not significant is lesser than the table value 1.98 with df 46 at 0.05 level. Hence, it is interpreted there is no significant difference on the mean values of academic factors responsible for the drop-outs among the male and female children at Primary level.

Table 5.6. Significance of difference of mean values of Academic factors responsible for drop-outs with respect to gender at Upper Primary Level

S. No.	Category	N	M	SD	T	Remarks
1.	Male	26	105	0.522	1.824	NSD
2.	Female	27	105.29	0.632		

Form the above table 5.6, the obtained 't' Value 1.824 is not significant is lesser than the table value 1.98 with df 46 at 0.05 level. Hence, it is revealed there is no significant difference on the mean values of academic factors responsible for the drop-outs among the male and female children at the Upper Primary level.

Table 5.7. Significance of difference of mean value of Academic factors responsible for drop-outs with respect to Community at Primary Level

S. No.	Category	N	M	SD	T	Remarks
1.	SC	21	105.84	1.308	0.653	NSD
2.	MBC / BC	26	105.58	1.335		

Form the above table 5.7, the obtained 't' Value 0.653 which df 46 is lesser than the table value 1.98 and is not significant 0.05 level. Hence, it is revealed there is no significance difference between the influence of SC community and backward, Most Backward community at Primary Level.

Table 5.8. Significance of difference of mean value of Academic factors responsible for drop-outs with respect to Community at Upper Primary Level

S. No.	Category	N	M	SD	T	Remarks
1.	SC	26	108.53	18.87	1.041	NSD
2.	MBC / BC	27	105.06	0.249		

Form the above table 5.8, the obtained 't' Value 1.041 which df 46 is lesser than the table value 1.98 and is not significant 0.05 level. Hence, it is revealed there was not significance difference between the influence of SC community and Backward, Most Backward community at Upper Primary Level.

Table 5.9. Significance of difference of mean value of Academic factors responsible for drop-outs with respect to Willing and Non-willing to go to school at Primary Level

S. No.	Category	N	M	SD	T	Remarks
1.	Willing to go to school	23	105.96	1.488	1.299	NSD
2.	Non-willing to go to school	24	105.46	1.079		

From the above table 5.9, the obtained 't' Value 1.299 with df 46 is lesser than the table value 1.98 and is not significant 0.05 level. Hence, it is understood there was no significance of difference between the influence of willing and non-willing to go to school at Primary Level.

Table 5.10. Significance of difference of mean value of Academic factors responsible for drop-outs with respect to Willing and Non-willing to go to school at Upper Primary Level

S. No.	Category	N	M	SD	T	Remarks
1.	Willing to go to school	29	105.24	0.625	0.972	NSD
2.	Non willing to go to school	24	105.08	0.571		

Form the above table 5.10, the obtained 't' Value 0.972 with df 46 is lesser than the table value 1.98 and is not significant 0.05 level. Hence, it is revealed there was no significance of difference between the influences of willing and non-willing to go to school at Upper Primary Level.

Table 5.11. Significance of difference of mean value of Academic factors responsible for drop-outs student at Primary Level

S. No.	Category	N	M	SD	T	Remarks
1.	Daily wages	26	106.09	1.234	3.075	SD
2.	Vendors	21	104.86	1.25		

From the above table 5.11, it was obtained 't' Value of 3.075 with df 46 is greater than the table value 1.98 and is significant at 0.05 level. Hence, it is concluded that there was significant difference between the influence of the daily wages and vendors at primary level. From the observed mean values it shows that mean values of daily wages activities is more influencing for drop-outs than vendors at Primary Level.

Table 5.12. Significance of difference of mean value of Academic factors responsible for dropouts with respect to nature of to work of the students at Upper Primary Level

S. No.	Category	N	M	SD	T	Remarks
1.	Daily wages	28	105.16	0.644	2.727	SD
2.	Vendors	25	105.25	0.433		

From the above table 5.12, it was revealed that the 't' Value of 2.727 with df 46 is greater than the table value 1.98 and is significant at 0.05 level. Hence, it is interpreted that there was significant difference between the influence of the daily wages and vendors at Upper Primary level. From the observed mean values it shows that mean values of Vendors is more influencing for drop-outs than daily wages at Upper Primary Level.

SECTION-D

Analysis of Economic Factors with Respect to Demographic Variables at Primary and Upper Primary Level

This section deals with the significance of difference of the mean values of Economic factors responsible for drop-outs with respect to gender that is male and female, community, willing and non-willing to go to school and nature of the work of the students at primary level and upper primary level.

Table 5.13. Significance of difference of mean value of Economic factors responsible for drop-outs with respect to gender at Primary Level

S. No.	Category	N	M	SD	T	Remarks
1.	Male	23	67.65	0.967	2.046	SD
2.	Female	24	67.03	1.048		

Form the above table 5.13, it was obtained 't' Value 2.046 is significant is greater than the table value 1.98 at

0.05 level. Hence, it is interpreted there is no significant difference on the mean values of Economic factors responsible for the dropouts among the male and female children at Primary level.

From the above table it is observed that meal value it shows that the mean value of male is more influencing than female at primary level.

Table 5.14. Significance of difference of mean values of Economic factors responsible for drop-outs with respect to gender at Upper Primary Level

S. No.	Category	N	M	SD	T	Remarks
1.	Male	26	69.95	0.475	1.341	NSD
2.	Female	27	69.74	0.67		

From the above table 5.14, the obtained 't' Value 1.341 is not significant is lesser than the table value 1.98 with df 46 at 0.05 level. Hence, it is revealed there is no significant difference on the mean values of Economic factors responsible for the drop-outs among the male and female children at the Upper Primary level.

Table 5.15. Significance of difference of mean value of Economic factors responsible for drop-outs with respect to Community at Primary Level

S. No.	Category	N	M	SD	T	Remarks
1.	SC	21	67.11	1.071	0.871	NSD
2.	MBC / BC	26	67.38	1.041		

From the above table 5.15, the obtained 't' Value 0.871 which df 46 is lesser than the table value 1.98 and is not significant 0.05 level. Hence, it is revealed that there was no significance difference between the influence of SC community and backward, Most Backward community at Primary Level.

Table 5.16. Significance of difference of mean value of Economic factors responsible for drop-outs with respect to Community at Upper Primary Level

S. No.	Category	N	M	SD	T	Remarks
1.	SC	26	76.91	12.49	0.738	NSD
2.	MBC/BC	27	70.27	0.998		

From the above table 5.16, the obtained 't' Value 0.738 which df 46 is lesser than the table value 1.98 and is not significant 0.05 level. Hence, it is interpreted that there was not significant of difference between the influence of SC community and Backward, Most Backward community at Upper Primary Level.

Table 5.17. Significance of difference of mean value of Economic factors responsible for drop-outs with respect to willing and Non-willing to go to school at Primary Level

S. No.	Category	N	M	SD	T	Remarks
1.	Willing to go to school	23	66.83	1.049	2.937	SD
2.	Non-willing to go to school	24	67.67	0.898		

From the above table 5.17, the obtained 't' Value 2.937 with df 46 is greater than the table value 1.98 and is not significant at 0.05 level. Hence, it is understood there was no significance of difference between the influence of willing and non-willing to go to school at Primary Level.

From the observed mean value it shows that the mean value of non-willing to go to school is more influencing than willing to go to school at Primary level.

Table 5.18. Significance of difference of mean value of Economic factors responsible for drop-outs with respect to Willing and Non-willing to go to school at Upper Primary Level

S. No.	Category	N	M	SD	T	Remarks
1.	Willing to go to school	29	69.83	0.647	0.25	NSD
2.	Non-willing to go to school	24	69.79	0.553		

From the above table 5.18, the obtained 't' Value 0.25 with df 46 is lesser than the table value 1.98 and is not significant at 0.05 level. Hence, it is revealed there was no significance of difference between the influence of willing and non-willing to go to school at Upper Primary Level.

Table 5.19. Significance of difference of mean value of Economic factors responsible for drop-outs with respect to nature of the work of the students at Primary Level

S. No.	Category	N	M	SD	T	Remarks
1.	Daily wages	26	66.91	1.042	5.294	SD
2.	Vendors	21	68.26	0.655		

From the above table 5.19, it was obtained 't' Value of 5.294 with df 46 is greater than the table value 1.98 and is significant at 0.05 level. Hence, it is concluded that there was significant difference between the influence of the daily wages and vendors at primary level.

From the observed mean values it showed that mean values of vendors is more influencing for drop-outs than daily wages at Primary Level.

Table 5.20. Significance of difference of mean value of Economic factors responsible for drop-outs with respect to nature of to work of the students at Upper Primary Level

S. No.	Category	N	M	SD	T	Remarks
1.	Daily wages	28	69.79	0.667	2.198	SD
2.	Vendors	25	70.5	0.866		

Form the above table 5.20, it was obtained 't' Value of 2.198 with df 46 is greater than the table value 1.98 and is significant at 0.05 level. Hence, it is interpreted that there was significant difference the influence of daily wages and vendors at Upper Primary level. From the observed mean values it shows that mean values of Vendors is more influencing than daily wages at Upper Primary Level.

SECTION-E

Analysis of Social Factors with Respect to Demographic Variables at Primary and Upper Primary Level

This section deals with the significance of difference of the mean values of Social factors responsible for drop-outs with respect to gender that is male and female, community, willing and non-willing to go to school and nature of the work of the students at primary level and upper primary level.

Table 5.21. Significance of difference of mean value of Social factors responsible for drop-outs with respect to gender at Primary Level

S. No.	Category	N	M	SD	T	Remarks
1.	Male	23	73.77	15.97	0.593	NSD
2.	Female	24	76.07	1.093		

From the above table 5.21, it was obtained 't' Value 0.593 is significant is lesser than the table value 1.98 with df 46 at 0.05 level. Hence, it is interpreted there is no significant difference on the mean values of Social factors responsible for the dropouts among the male and female children at Primary level.

Table 5.22. Significance of difference of mean values of Social factors responsible for drop-outs with respect to gender at Upper Primary Level

S. No.	Category	N	M	SD	T	Remarks
1.	Male	26	66.95	20.798	1.141	NSD
2.	Female	27	72.03	1.926		

From the above table 5.22, the obtained 't' Value 1.141 is not significant is lesser than the table value 1.98 with df 46 at 0.05 level. Hence, it is revealed there is no significant difference on the mean values of Social factors responsible for the drop-outs among the male and female children at the Upper middle level.

Table 5.23. Significance of difference of mean value of Social factors responsible for drop-outs with respect to Community at Primary Level

S. No.	Category	N	M	SD	T	Remarks
1.	SC	21	74.63	2.757	1.495	NSD
2.	MBC / BC	26	75.62	8.945		

From the above table 5.23, the obtained 't' Value 1.49 which df 46 is lesser than the table value 1.98 and is not significant 0.05 level. Hence, it is revealed that there was no significance difference between the influence of SC community and backward, Most Backward community at Primary Level.

Table 5.24. Significance of difference of mean value of Social factors responsible for drop-outs with respect to Community at Upper Primary Level

S. No.	Category	N	M	SD	T	Remarks
1.	SC	26	72.97	12.34	0.695	NSD
2.	MBC/BC	27	71.33	3.477		

From the above table 5.24, the obtained 't' Value 0.695 which df 46 is lesser than the table value 1.98 and is not significant 0.05 level. Hence, it is interpreted that there was no significant of difference between the influence of SC community and Backward, Most Backward community at Upper Primary Level.

Table 5.25. Significance of difference of mean value of Social factors responsible for drop-outs with respect to willing and Non-willing to go to school at Primary Level

S. No.	Category	N	M	SD	T	Remarks
1.	Willing to go to school	23	75.30	2.544	0.193	NSD
2.	Non-willing to go to school	24	75.42	1.579		

From the above table 5.25, the obtained 't' Value 0.193 with df 46 is Lesser than the table value 1.98 and is not significant 0.05 level. Hence, it is understood there was not significance of difference between the influence of willing and non-willing to go to school at Primary Level.

Table 5.26. Significance of difference of mean value of Social factors responsible for drop-outs with respect to Willing and Non-willing to go to school at Upper Primary Level

S. No.	Category	N	M	SD	T	Remarks
1.	Willing to go to school	29	71.03	3.189	0.214	NSD
2.	Non-willing to go to school	24	71.21	2.929		

From the above table 5.26, the obtained 't' Value 0.214 with df 46 is lesser than the table value 1.98 and is not significant at 0.05 level. Hence, it is revealed there was not significance of difference between the influence of willing and non-willing to go to school at Upper Primary Level.

Table 5.27. Significance of difference of mean value of Social factors responsible for drop-outs with respect to nature of the work of the students at Primary Level

S. No.	Category	N	M	SD	T	Remarks
1.	Daily wages	26	75.56	1.391	1.988	SD
2.	Vendors	21	75.14	3.09		

From the above table 5.27, it was obtained 't' Value of 1.988 with df 46 is greater than the table value 1.98 and is significant at 0.05 level. Hence, it is revealed that there was significant difference between the influence of the daily wages and vendors at primary level.

From the observed mean values it shows that mean values of daily wages is more influencing for drop-outs than vendors at Primary Level.

Table 5.28. Significance of difference of mean value of Social factors responsible for drop-outs with respect to nature of to work of the students at Upper Primary Level

S. No.	Category	N	M	SD	T	Remarks
1.	Daily wages	28	71.72	2.878	3.992	SD
2.	Vendors	25	67.88	2.421		

From the above table 5.28, it was obtained 't' Value of 3.992 with df 46 is greater than the table value 1.98 and is significant at 0.05 level. Hence, it is interpreted that there was significant difference the influence of daily wages and vendors at Upper Primary level.

From the observed mean values it shows that mean values of daily wages is more influencing for drop-outs than vendors at Upper Primary Level.

Findings, Suggestions and Conclusion

Chapter 6

OVERVIEW

The aim of the present study was to measure the reason of drop-outs among the Jeyankondam Union of Primary and Upper Primary Level children towards Academic, Economic and Social factors.

The attitude of drop-outs was measured through to the attitude scale consisting of 5 points such as strongly agree, agree, neutral, disagree and strongly disagree. The framed null-hypotheses were accepted of rejected based on the results derived from the analysis of Data.

This chapter presents the Findings of the study, Conclusions, Educational simplifications and suggestions for further study.

FINDINGS OF THE STUDY

The salient findings drawn from the analysis of the data under different sectors are given below:

Section A : Analysis on mean values at primary level and upper primary level.

Section B : Factor-wise analysis at primary level and upper primary level.

Section C : Analysis on Academic factors-wise respect to Demographic variables.

Section D : Analysis on Economic factors-wise respect to Demographic variables.

Section E : Analysis on Social factors-wise respect to Demographic variables.

Section A : Analysis on Mean Values

- The mean values of Academic factors fell in the range between 80 and 82, Economic factors fell in the range between 66 and 69 and social factors fell in the range between 55 and 59 in the primary level.
- It was understand from this that Academic factor stood first and then Economic and Social factors responsible for the drop-outs of children at primary level.
- In the upper primary level, the mean values of Academic factors fell in the range between 80 and 81, Economic factors fell in the range between 68 and 71 and Social factors fell in the range between 51 and 57.
- It was found that Academic factors stood first then Economic factors and Social Factors responsible for drop-outs of children at upper primary level.

Section B : Factor-wise Analysis at Primary and Upper Primary level

- Significant difference has been observed between Academic factors, Economic factors and Social factors. It was also found that the mean values of Academic factors was more influencing in the drop-outs of primary level children.
- Similarly in the upper primary level too, the significant difference has been observed between Academic factors, Economic factors and Social factors. It was also found that the mean values of Academic factors was more influences in the drop-outs of upper primary level children.

- It was found that the significant difference between Academic factors *vs* Economic factors and Academic factors *vs* Social Factors in the dropouts of primary level children.
- It was also found that the significant difference between Academic factors *vs* Economic factors and Academic factors *vs* Social factors But not wish Economic factors *vs* Social factors in the dropouts of upper primary level children.
- It was also found that Academic factors was more influencing than Economic factors and Social factors where as Economic factors and Social factors are found to be similar.

Section C : Analysis on Academic factors with respect to demographic variables at primary and upper primary level.

- It was found that there was no significant difference on the mean values of Academic factors responsible for drop-outs among the male and female children at primary level.
- Similarly in the upper primary level, there was no significant difference on the mean values of Academic factors responsible for drop-outs among the male and female children.
- It was found that there was no significance of difference between the influence of SC Community and BC/MBC community at Primary level.
- Similarly in the Upper Primary level, there was significance of difference between the influence of SC Community and MBC / BC community.
- It was understood there was no significance of difference between the influence of willing and non-willing to go to school at Primary level.
- Similarly in the Upper Primary level, it was found that there was significance of difference between the influence of willing and non-willing to go to school.

- There was significance of difference between the influence of daily wages and vendors at Primary level.

  From the observed mean values it shows that mean values of drop-outs engaging in Daily wages was more influencing for dropouts engaging in vendors at Primary level.

- Similarly, in the Upper Primary level, there was significance of difference between the influence of drop-outs engaging in daily wages and vendors.

  From the observed mean values it shows that mean values of dropouts engaging in vendors was more influencing for drop-outs than drop-outs engaging in daily wages at Upper Primary level.

Section D : Analysis on Economic Factors with Respect to Demographic Variables at Primary and Upper Primary Level

- It was found that significant difference on the mean values of Economic factors responsible for the drop-outs among the male and female children at primary level.

  From the observed mean values it shows that the mean value of male was more influencing than female at primary level.

- In the Upper Primary level, there was no significance of difference on the mean value of Economic factors responsible for the drop-outs among the male and female children.
- It was found that there was no significance of difference between the influence of SC community and MBC/BC community at Primary level.
- Similarly, in the Upper Primary level there was significance of difference between the influence of SC Community and MBC/BC community.
- It was understood that there was significance of difference between the influence of willing and non-

willing to go to school among drop-outs Primary level. From the observed mean values it shows that the mean value of non-willing to go to school was more influencing than willing to go to school at among drop-outs primary level.

- But in the Upper Primary level, there was no significance of difference between the influence of willing and non-willing to go to school among drop-outs children.
- It was found that there was significance of difference between the influence of daily wages and vendors at primary level.

  From the observed mean values it shows that mean value of drop-outs engaging vendors it was more influencing for drop-outs than daily wages at primary level.
- Similarly, in the Upper Primary level, there was significance of difference between the influence of drop-outs engaging in daily wages and vendors. From the observed mean values it shows that the mean values of drop-outs engaging in vendors was more influencing than drop-outs engaging in daily wages at Upper Primary level.

Section E : Factor-wise Analysis at Primary and Upper Primary Level

- It was found that there was no significance of difference on the mean values of social factors responsible for the drop-outs among the male and female children at Primary level.
- Similarly, in the Upper Primary level it was found that there was no significance of difference on the mean values of social factors responsible for drop-outs among the male and female children.
- It was found that there was no significance of difference between the influence of SC community and BC/ MBC community at Primary level.
- Similarly, in the Upper Primary level, It was found that there was no significance of difference between

the influence of SC Community and BC/MBC community.

- It was found that there was not significance of difference between the influence of willing and non-willing to go to school at Primary level.
- Similarly in the Upper Primary level, It was found that there was no significance of difference between the influence of willing and non-willing to go to school among drop-outs.
- It was found that there was significance of difference between the influence of drop-outs engaging at daily wages and vendors at Primary level. From the observed mean values it shows that the mean value of drop-outs engaging in daily wages was more influencing than dropouts engaging in vendors at primary level.
- Similarly, in the Upper Primary level, it was found that there was significance of difference between the influence of drop-outs engaging in daily wages and vendors. From the observed mean values it shows that the mean values of drop-outs engaging in daily wages was more influencing than drop-outs engaging in vendors at Upper Primary level.

DISCUSSION OF THE STUDY

It was understood from the perusal of the study that all the drop-outs children irrespective of sex, community, willing and non-willing to go to school and present their occupation were having the favourable attitude to the range of around 75 per cent towards Academic, Economic, and Social factors. It shows that they are having good option towards the above variables. This may be due to the fact that the students have become drop-outs children not because of interest, but because of some other compulsions.

Though all the children having favourable attitude towards drop-outs children, there was some difference when the analysis was made between certain variables.

It was reported that positively high significant was observed among Academic and Economic factor than Social factors at primary and Upper Primary level. It is inferred from the fact that students will behave normally when there are given equal education opportunities.

It was reported that positively high significant difference was observed among drop-outs engaging in daily wages than drop-outs engaging vendors activities at Primary and Upper Primary level.

It was reported that positively high significant difference of Economic factors was observed among boys than girls at Primary level. But the Primary level there was no significant difference between boys and girls.

It was reported that positively high significant difference between willing and non-willing to go to school in Primary level. The drop-outs children at Primary level willing to go to school is more than non-willing to go to school. But the Upper Primary level there was no significant difference between willing and non-willing to go to school.

The significant difference among the drop-outs may be more educational awareness among the boys at Primary level and Upper Primary level.

CONCLUSION OF THE STUDY

It is concluded from the findings that all the children are having favourable attitude towards the drop-outs children. The same trend in the attitude was observed when the sample was classified with respect to sex, community, willing and non-willing to go to school and wish respect to nature of the work of the drop-outs children at Primary and Upper Primary level. When the analysis was made between the variables it was observed that the attitudes towards "Academic factors" and "Economic factors" were more than other variables such as "Social factor".

REFERENCES

1. Bhatnagar, Suresh. *Indian Education Today and Tomorrow.* Meerut: Internation, 1983 pp. 124-148.
2. Bihari., L.R., (1969). *Wastage and Stagnation in Primary Education Among the Tribals,* Tribal Research and Training Institute, Gujarat Vidyapeeth. Ahmedabad, Buch, M.B., Third Survey of Research in Education (1978-83), p. 133.
3. Cervantes., L.F. *The Drop-outs : Causes and Cures,* Ann Arbor: Michigan Press, 1965.
4. Cohen, S.B., and Betten Court, L.U. (1991). Drop-out: Intervening with Reluctant Learner, Intervention in School and Clinic. In *Sociological Abstract.* 42 (I). 1994. p. 178.
5. Conger, J.J. and Peterson, C.A. *Adolescence and Youth,* Third ed. New York : Harper and Row, 1984. pp. 146, 148, 152, 425.
6. Contractor, B.M., (1977) Educational Attainment as a Function of Certain Variables. Ph.D., Psy. Gujarat U., Buch, M.B. Third Survey of Research in Education. (1978-83). p. 661.
7. Crow, L.D. and Crow, L. *Educational Psychology.* New Delhi: Eurasia. 1962, pp. 145-146.
8. Dass, J.R and Grag, V.P. (1985): Impact of Preprimary Education on Drop-outs, Stagnation and Academic Performance, Education Department, Municipal Corporation, Delhi. Buch, M.B. *Fourth Survey of Research in Education* (1983-88). Vol. II, p. 1265.
9. Das, D.C. (1969). A Study of the Wastage and Stagnation at the Elementary Level of Education in the State of Assam with Special Reference to the Primary Stage, SIE. Assam, Buch, M.B., *Fourth Survey of Research in Education* (1983-88).
10. Das R.C. (1979). Effectiveness of Teacher Training in Reducing Educational Wastage. SIE, Assam, Buch, M.B., *Fourth Survey of Research in Education* (1983-88) Vol. II, p. 930.
11. Das R.C. (1975). A Comparative Study of Educational Wastage in Urban and Rural Areas. SIE, Assam, Buch, M.B., *Fourth Survey of Research in Education* (1983-88) Vol. II, p. 1263.
12. Delores, Jaques. (1996). *Learning : The Treasure Within.* Report to UNESCO of the International Commission for the 21st Century.
13. Davies, Scott (1994). In Search of Resistance and Rebellion Among High School Drop-outs. *Canadian Journal of Sociology* 19(3). 331-350. In Sociological Abstract (1995). 43 (2).

14. Devi, K.G. (1983). Problem of Dropouts in Primary Schools of Manipur with Special Reference to Imphal Town (1963-1970). Ph.D.Edu.Gau, U.Buch, M.B., *Fourth Survey of Research in Education* (1983-88). Vol. II, p. 1267.
15. Figueira, Mc Donough, Josefina (1992). Community Contex and Drop-outs Rates School Social Work Arizona State Univ. Children and Youth Services Review: In Sociological Abstract. 41(2).
16. Flisher, A.J., and Chalton, D.O. (1995). High School Dropouts in a Working Class South African Community: Selected Characteristics and Risk Taking Behaviour. *Journal of Adolescent*. Feb., 105-121. In sociological Abstract. 43 (5), 1995.
17. Franklin, C. and Streeter, C.L. (1995). Assessment of Middle Class Youth At Risk to Drop-outs School, Psychological and Family Correlates. *Children and Youth Services Review, 17,* 433-488.
18. Garcia de Vicens et al., (1979). Measurement of School Drop-outs in Argentina. Revista Paraguaya de Scoiologia, 16, 45. In Sociological Abstract. 29 (4), 1991.
19. Gogate, S.B. (1982), A Critical Study of the Drop-outs at the +2 Stage (New XI & XII) in Raigad (Kolaba) District Maharashtra. Buch., M.B., *Third Survey of Research in Education* (1978-83).
20. Gupta, S.L., (1974). A Study of the Impact of the Ungraded School System on Reducing School Drop-outs and Stagnation in Primary Schools (1970-74). NCERT. New Delhi.
21. Hussain, M., (1982) Wastage and Stagnation in Primary School of Rural Areas of Bhilwara District. SIERT, Rajasthan, Buch, M.B., *Fourth Survey of Research in Education* (1983-88) Vol.II, p. 1272.
22. Jordan, Will J., Lara and Mc Partland James (1996). Exploring the Causes of Early Drop-outs Among Race, Ethnic and Gender Groups. *Youth and Society,* 28, 62-94.
23. Joshi, N.D., (1981), Problems Faced by Certain Tribal Groups in Trivandrum District in Relation to Provision and Use of school Facilities. Dept. of Edu., Ker. U. Buch., M.B. *Third survey of Research in Education* (1978-83). pp. 78-83.
24. Kasen, Stephanie; Cohen Patricia and Brook, Judith S. (1998). Adolescent School Experiences and Drop-outs, Adolescent Pregnancy, and Young Adult Deviant Behaviour. *Journal of Adolescent Research.* 13, 49-72. In Child Development Abstract and Bibliography, 72 (2).
25. Kasinath, H.M. (1980). A Critical Study of the Problems of Wastage and Stagnation in Primary Education in Karnataka State. Ph.D., Edu. Kar. U., Buch., M.B. Third Survey of Research in Education (1978-83) p. 911.

26. Khandeker, M. (1974). A Study of Drop-outs. TISS, Bombay, Buch., M.B., Second Survey of Research in Education (1972-73).
27. Khana, K. (1983). Preparation of Reading Material for Girl Drop-outs in Delhi Slums. Ph.D., Edu, Del.U., Buch., M.B., Fourth Survey of Research in Education (1983-88). Vol. II p. 597.
28. Leslie F. Hale, Ed. D., NCSP, et al., (1998). School Drop-outs Prevention : Information and Strategies for Educators, National Association of School Psychologists, 4340 East-West Highway, Suit 402, Betehrsder MD 20814.
29. Mathur, J.S., Jain, S.P., and Rahim, C.A. (1982). Rural Youths from Poverty Groups, Drop-outs and Non-students : A Study for Four States. NIRD, Buch, M.B., Fourth Survey of Research in Education (1983-88). Vol I, p. 169.
30. Masavi, M. (1976). Wastage and Stagnation in Primary Education in Tribal Areas. Tribal Research and Training Institute. Gujarat Vidyapith, Ahmedabad, Buch., M.B., *Third Survey of Research in Education* (1978-83), p. 154.
31. McCaul, J.Edward. *et al.* (1992) Consequences of Dropping out of School : Findings from High School and Beyond. *Journal of Education Research.* Washington, D.C : 1992, 85 (4), pp. 198-207.
32. McNeal, Ralph, Barners, Jr (1994). Dropping out of High School : Individual and School Variation. *Dissertation Abstracts International, The Humanities and Social Sciences,* 55(6), 1524-A.
33. McNeal, Ralph, B. Jr. (1995) Extracurricular Activities and High School Drop-outs. Un *Sociology of Education,* 68. In Sociological Abstract 43 (3).
34. Nail., C. (1981). A Survey of Drop-outs and Non-enrolment of Children in the 6-14 Age Group. Indian Institute of Education, Pune. *Third Survey of Research in Education* (1978-83), p. 916.
35. National Drop-outs Prevention Centre at Clemson University; 205 Martin Street, Clemson, SC 29634-5111 : (803) 656-2599; http\\www.dropoutprevention.org.
36. Nayal, G.S. and Nayal, S. (1989). Differential Personality Profiles of High School Drop-outs and Stay-ins. *Indian Educational Review.* 24(3), 103-109. In Fifth Survey of Research in Education (1988-92). Vol. I, p. 324.
37. Pellas, A.M., (1987). School Drop-outs in the United States, Washington DC: Center for Education Statistics. (ERIC Document Reproduction Services N.Ed., 283119).
38. Pillai, G.V. Benjamin, J. and Mair, K.R., (1980). A Study of Drop-outs in Primary Education in Kerala. State Planning Board, Government of Kerala, Trivandrum, Buch, MB. *Third Survey of Research in Education* (1978-83). p. 932.

39. Punalekar, S.P. (1975). School Drop-outs among Harijan Children, Causes and Cure. Central Institute of Research and Training in Public Co-operation New Delhi. Buch., M.B., *Third Survey of Research in Education* (1978-83). p. 175.

40. Rumberger, R.W., (1983). Dropping Out of High School: The Influence of Race, Sex and Family Background. *American Education Research Journal.* 20. 199-200.

41. Sarkar, B.N. (1980), A Pilot Investigation on School Drop-outs Reasons. Demography Research Unit. ISI, Calcutta. Buch., M.B., Third Survey of Research in Education (1978-83) p. 948.

42. Setharamu, A.S. and Ushadevi, M.D. (1981). School Drop-outs in Rural Areas : A Study of the Drop-outs in Karnataka State. Institute for Social and Economic Change. Bangalore, Buch., M.B., *Third Survey of Research in Education* (1978-83). p. 197.

43. Sharma, R.C. and Sapra. C.L., 1969. Wastage and Stagnation in Primary and Middle Schools in India. NCERT, New Delhi.

44. SIE (U.P.) (1968) A Study of Dropouts and Failures in Primary Classes, Allahabad, Buch, M.B., Fourth Survey of Research in Education (1983-88) Vol. II., p. 1281.

45. Srivastava, S. and Gupta, A.P. (1980). Survey of the Non-enrolled, Non-attending and Drop-outs Children of the Age Group (6-14) in the Ferozepore District. Dev. Samaj College of Education for Women, Ferozepore District. Dev.Samaj College of Education for Women, Ferozpore, Buch, M.B., *Third Survey of Research in Education* (1978-83), p. 972.

46. Vathsala, S. (1981). Potential Drop-outs at Middle School Level. Ph.D., Edu. Madras U., Buch M.B., *Third Survey of Research in Education* (1978-83).

JOURNALS

- Indian Journal of Social Work. Vol.22, No.4 January 1972, Working Children in Greater Bombay by Khandekar Mandakini and Naik, M.D.
- Lok. Kalyan, Vol. 2 No. 1., Jan-1979, Poverty Main Cause of children's and Employment by Kusum.
- Main Stream, June 1980, Poverty Breeding Ground for Child Labour by Mohsini.
- Social Welfare, Vol. 23 No. 8 1976, "Children Are Working In Millions" by Seongupta P.
- Social Change, Vol. 2, No. 3 September 1972, Protection for the Child by Baig Tara, A1.

AWARENESS IN ICT

Introduction

Chapter 7

Introduction

The present study entitled *"Awareness on ICT's Among P.G. Teacher in Higher Secondary Schools"* aims at finding out the awareness of P.G. Teachers towards using modern technologies in class room instruction. In today's fast paced technological scene, it is crucial for a student to be able to adapt to new technologies fast. The information technology or IT is revolutionising the way in which we live and work. It is changing all aspects of our life style. To survive in this information world, one must keep pace with these changes.

Dr. A.P.J. Abdul Kalam has pointed out that our educational system should develop certain capacities like inquiry, creativity entrepreneurial and moral leadership in the learners, so that they will be able to face and facilitate there participation in the task of national development. Information and communication technology has brought many ways to develop these capacities. Hence the teachers should be competent enough to conduct and facilitate learning through the recent developments in technology.

MEANING AND CONCEPT OF EDUCATIONS

Education is the process by which and through which the experience of knowledge, skills and attitudes are transmitted to the members of the community. According to Encyclopaedia (1988) "Education is a process by which people acquire knowledge, skills, habits and values or attitudes". Education can help a person to understand social changes and provide the skills for adjusting to them. Education involves many activities directed towards the development of overall personality of human being.

The great Indian philosopher Mahatma Gandhi has correctly said "By Education, I mean an all round drawing out of the best in child and man body, mind and spirit." "Education is the manifestation of divine perfection, already exiting in man"—Swami Vivekananda.

DEVELOPMENT OF EDUCATION TECHNOLOGY

The information age clearly makes new demands on the educational system, requiring radical changes in what and how people learn. Many educators believe that computers and information technology are essential parts of these changes.

MEANING OF EDUCATIONAL TECHNOLOGY

Educational Technology implies a behavioural science approach to teaching and learning in make use of pertinent scientific and technological methods and concepts developed in psychology, sociology, communications, linguistics and other related fields. Educational technology is the development, application and evaluation of system, techniques and aids to improve the purpose of human learning.

Kulkarni (1989) considered Educational technology as an instrument which can be used for both developments in a narrow sense or reconstruction in a holistic sense. It is the designer of the system of Educational Technology who has to formulate the goals very specifically and then build the strategy to achieve those goals. Galbraith defines Educational Technology as a systematic application of scientific or other organised knowledge of practical task.

Role of Technology in Education

The National Policy on Education (1986) assigned an important role to Educational Technology for improving the quality of education. The purpose for which educational technology is to be employed includes spread of useful information, the training and retraining of teachers to improve quality, sharpen awareness of art and culture, inculcate abiding values etc. both in formal and informal sectors.

Educational Technology should help to improve the overall efficiency of the learning and teaching process. Technology in education has seen many successes. It is the ingenuity of teachers who saw great potential in various technologies and adopted them to their advantages. Technology is meant to help as excel in whatever we are doing, improving our efficiency even make out life easier perhaps.

Statement of the Problem

The problem selected for the present study is "Awareness on ICT's among P.G Teachers in Higher Secondary Schools". The investigator attempts to study the Awareness of P.G. Teachers on ICT's.

Attitude

Attitude is mental and natural state or realness, organized through experiences exerting a directive or dynamic influence upon the individual's response to objects and situation with which help he is related to. Attitude values and ideas that are propagated by education play an important significance role in building the personality, individuality and the entire mental make-up of an individual. It is a guiding force behind all human action.

According to Thurstone (1974) the term denotes the sum total of man's inclination and feelings, prejudices or bias preconceived ideas, fears, threats and convictions about any specified topic.

The major characteristics of attitude are:

(*i*) Attitudes are related with images and external objects;

(*ii*) Attitudes guide the behaviours of individual in one particular direction;

(*iii*) Various kinds of affective experiences are also attached to attitude;

(*iv*) The unconscious motive is an important vector in the creation of attitude.

(*v*) Attitudes are related to the persons needs and problems.

In a nutshell attitude is specific mental state of the individual towards something according to which his behavior is molded.

COMPUTERS IN SCHOOLS

The information age clearly makes new demands on the educational system, requiring radical changes in what and how people learn. Many educators believe that computers and information technology are essential parts of the changes. Many of the elementary and secondary schools are now introducing computers. Students and teachers are using this computer in a variety of ways to learn.

Advantages of Computers in Instruction

Computers allow students to learn based on drill and practice principle. The computer based training allows students to learn at their own pace, in small step and give feedback about how much they have learned.

• **Computer aided Instruction** is one of the most commonly used educational software. It is relatively easy and inexpensive to produce, it can easily be combined with more traditional educational techniques and it produces clear, demonstrable results CAI offers many advantages.

• **Individualised learning** individual student can learn at his own pace. Teachers can spend time working one-on-

one with students—an important activity that is almost impossible in typical presentation—and-discussion class rooms.

- **Motivation** CAI can turn practice in to an entertaining game it motivates students to practice arithmetic, spelling and other skills that might otherwise be tedious to learn.

- **Confidence** CAI can help timid children become comfortable with computer as well as with the subject matter being taught Research has soon that younger children, disadvantaged children and especially learning disabled student tend to respond positively to CAI.

OBJECTIVE OF THE STUDY

The major objective of the study is to find out the awareness on ICT's among P.G Teachers in Higher Secondary School.

The other specific objectives are given below:-

1. To find out the awareness of rural and urban P.G Teachers towards ICT's.
2. To find out the awareness of male and female P.G Teachers towards ICT's.
3. To find out the awareness of P.G Teachers of different discipline such as arts and science.
4. To find out the awareness of P.G Teachers of different qualifications such as M.Phil, B.Ed, M.Ed.
5. To find out the awareness of P.G Teachers working in Government, Aided and Self-financing institutions.
6. To find out the awareness of P.G Teachers on ICT's possessing or not possessing computer knowledge.

NEED FOR THE STUDY

In order to bring effective improvement in the quality of education it is necessary to focus attention on the new technologies. One such recent and most dominating technology is computer technology. Computer plays great revolution in every walks of life. But when we think about its development in the field of education, it is only in an infant stage. Now many people start thinking to add computer education in curriculum at all possible ways. Hence it is important to study the awareness on ICT's among P.G Teachers.

SCOPE OF STUDY

The investigator attempted to know the awareness of P.G Teachers on ICT's. The study will be of great help for the educationists particularly for the teachers since the concept of education has been changing from time to time. The attitude may be different from person to person. One can learn and do anything with involvement only when he had a better attitude towards it. In this content the investigator attempts to study the influence and awareness of using modern technology among P.G Teachers in classroom instruction.

LIMITATIONS OF THE STUDY

Broadly speaking any study in impossible. This study too has some limitations.

- The investigator was unable to investigate many P.G teachers. The study was confined to only 200 P.G Teachers.
- The present study was restricted to P.G Teachers only.
- The study was concerned with awareness of variables such as locality, sex, and academic qualification, type of institution and knowledge of computer.

Chapter 8

Review of Related Literature

Introduction

Review of related literature besides allowing the researcher to acquaint himself with current knowledge in the field or area in which the research is being conducted, serve the following purpose :

- To delete the limits of field of study.
- To avoid unfruitful and useless problem areas.
- To avoid unintentional duplication of well established findings.
- To understand research methodology which refers to the way in which the study is to be conducted.
- To know about the recommendations of previous researches listed in their studies for future research.

Investigator conducted a close study of researches done in area of ICT's as instructional technology.

Need for the Related Literature

A review of the previous investigations is necessary to gain better perspective of the problem. The review of related studies is necessary to show whether the evidence already solve the problem adequately with investigation to avoid the risk of duplication of idea, explanations, or hypothesis, variable in formulating the problem, to suggest methods of research appropriate to the problem, to get an idea about the current trend in the field and so on. The survey of literature is a crucial aspect of the planning if the study and the time spent in the survey invariably a wise investment. Hence an attempt was made to the review the studies conducted in India and aboard.

CLASSIFICATION OF THE STUDIES

The total studies identified are classified under two captions. One is studies conducted in India and another one in abroad.

Studies Conducted in India

The investigator identified 30 studies the satellite Instructional Television Experiment. The objective of the study were to study the social and economic context of the target audience in term of dimensions relevant to rural development television, to study the social dynamics of the introduction of TV in relatively backward areas, to study whether those who were attracted towards TV, to study the TV viewing behaviour of those who watched the satellite Instructional Television Experiment (SITE) programme more or less regularly, to study how far SITE has been able to attract its target audience, to assess the relevance and impact of the instructional programme in terms of needs of the audience. The study adopted one village for intensive study and four villages for survey. In the intensive study, informal discussion, family set-up in the village interpersonal communication, and functioning of social, religious and political institutions were studied after 5 months of the commencement of the programme, the subject who said that they viewed the programmed daily (N=75) and those who said they rarely viewed it (N=75) were selected. The viewers and non-viewers were given a knowledge test about agriculture. The data were also collected through interviews about social participation, outside visit, interaction with development officials, modernity and awareness about agriculture innovations. The findings were less than one-fourth of the heads of households were found to be regular viewers; the presentation of most of the programmers of TV lacks the local touch. Through the language used was Hindi, there was inadequate participation and involvement of local organisations and agencies because of the absence of a process which should have made all feel their role as participants, there was insistence on from rather than content in the programmers.

Ediger (1987) studied the use of "Micro Computers in the Class Room". From this study he found that computer helps optimum student's achievement. The main objectives of this study were to provide meaningful experience to learn and provide sequential learning. The study revealed that the audio-visual materials need to be utilised as learning both in microcomputer and traditional reading to attain worthwhile goal, so that learners may perceive meaning, purpose and interest in learning.

A comparative study was carried out by *Chandra* (1987) on using computer Assisted instruction and close circuit Television for Instruction in science for ninth standard pupils. The sample consisted of 10 boys and 10 girls. Pre, post tests experimental design was followed. From the analysis of the scores obtained by the students, it was found that 95 per cent of the students had answered 85 per cent of the computer assisted instruction questions correctly. Similarly *Natchimuthu (1989)* revealed that CAI students scored Significantly well and participated enthusiastically.

Karpaga Kumaravel (1990) in his study on the effectiveness of computer assisted instruction, video assisted instruction and conventional instruction in English language learning found the achievement of video assisted instruction group is better than computer assisted instruction and conventional instructional group.

Sanasanwal and Anuradha (1990) found the effectiveness of instructional strategy in terms of higher mental ability. The experiment was carried out for a period of the 75 working days and involved instruction of five units in physics. The main limitation as expressed by some students is the lack of interaction with living tissues. The conclusion was the CAL is an interesting and useful educational tool to demonstrate drug effects on living tissues and animals.

Shajahan (1990) proved that modular way of learing was more effectiveness than the convential methods. An overwhelming majority of the students possessed a favourable attitude towards modular instruction and achievement of students was also increased after the modules taught to them.

Goel (1991) studied on the "Development of computer based evaluation software on Educational Technology for M.Ed". The objectives were to develop computer based evaluation software on educational technology and to study the reactions of students towards computerized testing. The important findings revealed that the computer based evaluation was objective, valid, reliable and comprehensive. It was efficient and well organised, reduced the work load of teachers and could be used and again. To conclude that computer is a very suitable medium for resting. Hardware expensive is quite accepted in our country but there is need to develop suitable software to utilise it.

Regser (1991) conducted a study on effects of computer education on student's achievement, attitude and self esteem'. This study was designed to examine the effects of computer education of student's achievement attitude and self esteem and investigate the relationship between success with computer instruction and personality characteristics, IQ, age and attitude towards school.

The major findings of the study are:

- There were interesting students gain ineffective areas such as attitude and self esteem. Students receiving computer instruction agreed more strongly with positive attitude statements.

- There were no sex related differences in achievement attitude and personality characteristics.

Mayur and Mohite (1992) study pointed out that in Indian, children constitute not only 40 percentage of the total TV audience but numerically, and physically, spent more time in front of the television set than adults. They indicated that TV viewers of the elementary school developed interests and improved their skills in many co-curricular activities. Further, the study revealed that the exposure to TV is of cognitive in nature. The TV influence different aspects positive or negative depending upon the quality programmers and characteristics of audience.

Elmore (1992) made an analysis of the fifty-one computer modules designed to enhance the knowledge skills and attitudes needs by teacher education student', reactions to a set of 51 computers modules called performance Element Module (PEMS). These modules focussed on selected knowledge skills and attitude needed by teacher education students. The main objective was to assess whether students will accepts the 51 computer assigned modules as viable instructional tools.

The major finding revealed means scores mean scores of 7.73 for user friendliness, of computer. For involvement and interaction of the computer programme (Modules) a mean scores of 7.3 was repeated. Did the modules help students correct a lack of information or improve the skill? A mean of the 7.12 was reported which was interpreted as an indication that the modules were visible instructional aids.

One was *Anadan, K.* (1992) studied the effect of CAI on achievement in Indian Economics among Higher Secondary students. The major objective of the study was to find out the effectiveness of CAI in Indian Econamics of the 11th Class English medium students. The design of the study was per-post equality group design. The experimental group-I consisted of 129 students and experimental group-II consisted of 14 students. There were 34 students into control group. The study found that the control group students stay behind significantly from experimental group-I and experimental group-II in their achievement in Indian Economics for the two components, namely, knowledge and comprehension. But for the component of application, no significant difference was observed between the pairs of the samples group of students.

Ravindranath (1993) studied on the "computers in DIETS". The important objective of the study was to bring about a quantitative improvement in the educational system. It points out the influence in the field of computer systems, and has witnessed a number of innovations in the last two decades. Because of these innovations, today, computers have remained no more a sophisticated calculator or typewriter. The computers are being used to handle large volumes of spiral and non-spiral data strategic manipulation analysis and retrieval.

An investigation was made by *Singh, J.K.,* (1993) on the topic "Integrating Computers in Education". The main objectives of the study were:

(*i*) To provide prospective teachers with basic information about the range of computer applications.

(*ii*) To identify ways the computer may improve the teaching learning process.

(*iii*) To introduce and build on the concept of the integrating computers in the classroom.

(*iv*) To emphasise the idea of co-operative learning culture within a technological environment.

The study concluded that it is important that technology be used to help children think critically and creatively and to promote a co-operative learning environment. By teaching the education students to use technology wisely, it is hoped that future teachers will successfully incorporate technology into their classrooms.

Beena and Aggarwal (1994) conducted a study entitled. "Teachers Attitude Towards Computer Assisted Instruction and Computer Education in to Sex Organisation and Experience". The main objectives of the study were know the relationship between gander and attitude towards computer education and computer assisted instruction, and to study the relationship between teaching experiences. They concluded that the female teachers had more positive attitude than public school teachers.

Siva Kumar, Arun Kumar and Sundaramurthy (1994) conducted a study on "Effectiveness of computer assisted instruction, laboratory centered instruction and conventional classroom teaching in technical education". The objective of the study was to compare the relative effectiveness of CAI, LCI and classroom teaching in term of the achievement of polytechnic students.

The main finding was that direct learning experience given through laboratory centered instruction is far superior to self instructional strategy and conventional classroom teaching. As students remembered the experience gained through the direct experience for a longer period of time, it was recommended that the teachers adopt such strategies in regular classroom teaching.

Wagh, (1995) developed a multimedia instructional system for remedial purpose for fractional numbers and found that this package led to better understanding than the conventional remedial methods.

An investigation was made by *Reddy and Ramer* (1995) to assess the "Effectiveness of computer assisted instruction in teaching sciences to slow learners". The main objectives of the study were:

(*i*) To find out whether there is any significant difference between the pre-test and post-test mean scores of the slow learners in the control group.

(*ii*) To assess whether there exits any significant difference between the present and post-test mean scores of the slow learners in the experimental group.

(*iii*) To find out whether there is any significant difference between the post-test mean scores of the experimental group and the control group.

(*iv*) To assess whether there exits any significant difference between the post-test mean scores of the slow learners in the group and the students in the normal group.

The main finding of the study was that significant difference was found between the post test mean scores of the experimental group slow learners and the normal group students. The achievement of normal group student was higher than the achievement of experimental group slow learner, the gap between both the groups was reduced to a great extent. This can be ascribed to the effectiveness of CAI.

Reddey and Ramar (1995) studied that the larger gap between both control and experimental group was reduced in favour of experimental group which was due to the effect of CAI.

Kumar (1996) studied about the use of technology in education resulting in increased effectiveness of educational process. Each new physical prescribes the uses of procedures and techniques. The uses of technology increase productivity too, enhancing the human capability.

Amirtharaj (2001) studied the attitude of B.Ed Trainees of Sri Rama Krishna Mission Vidyalaya collage of education towards computer in Education. According to this study, the researcher analysed the attitude of the B.Ed trainees towards the computer in education, the necessarily to giving importance to computer education to the B.Ed trainees to find out with respect to their interest towards computer based on optional subjects and to find to differences with respect to the subject whether in their towards the computer in education were done.

Kuruvilla. A (2001) studied the use of computer Assisted Learning as an adjuvant to practical pharmacology teaching; advantages and limitations. Their objectives are: to assess the student's acceptability of computer Assisted Learning (CAL) as a method of demonstrating drug effects in animals and to receive feedback CAL software from two sources were used to demonstrate action of drugs in animals. Feedback was obtained from student regarding the acceptability, advantages and limitations of this method. The results of the study were; majority of the students expressed the opinion that cal is an effective a method of teaching practical aspects of technology. Twenty-three classroom teachers were surveyed to determine their use of computers for themselves and as teaching tools for their students.

Umme Kulsum (2002) conducted a study on "Teachers attitude towards computer". The findings of the study revealed that primary and secondary School teachers had more favourable attitude towards computer and there was no significance difference between them.

Balasubramaniam and Jayaraman (2002) explored to find out the "Relative effectiveness among different modes of computer based instruction". An attempt was made in this study to establish the effectiveness among tutorial, drill and proactive and stimulation as different modes of computer based instruction in realising the instructional as well as to enhance the relation of what has been already learnt in the context of teaching modern physics at higher secondary stage. Present, post-test, non-equivalent group design was adopted in conducting the experiment.

Bala Ayyappan (2003) conducted a study on "B.Ed student's attitude towards the use of computer". The study that gender of students caused significance with respect to their attitude towards the use of computer, but the locale and educational qualifications did not cause significance difference with respect to their attitude towards the use of computer.

Manoharan V (2005) conducted a study on certain personal variable as related to classroom climate and teachers teaching effectiveness as perceived by higher secondary students. To find out of there is any significant difference in classroom climate as perceived by student. The Simple Random Sampling Method is adapted for ten schools of Dindigul district. By using the simple random sampling technique 410-second year students were used for this study among them, 200 were boys and 210 were girls. In the study there is no significant difference in classroom climate as perceived by the student in term of sex. That is, girls perceived more classroom climate that boy. Girls are generally more disciplined than boys, perhaps this may be the reason for this finding, in the study there is no significant difference in teaching effectiveness as perceived by students in terms of caste, native place and type of family and size of family.

Nachimuthu K. (2005) conducted a study on CAI on leaves. The objectives of the study were, to develop and validate the CAI material in Biology subject, particularly in 'Leaves'. He took the sample were 60 in two different higher secondary schools of Erode district of Tamil Nadu; He developed the martial by visual Basic software in the computer. He concluded that the CAI was slightly effective than the classroom achievement. And also he strongly concluded that the CAI was used the mastery level of the subjectivity, particularly in Biology.

Nirmala S. (2005) studied the "Attitude towards computer education of the B.Ed. Trainees of Tamilnadu Open University. The sample for the present study consisted of 60 B.Ed trainees. The investigator had developed a tool to measure attitude towards computer education. The data were analysed by using mean, SD and "t" test. The finding revealed that the B.Ed students of Tamil Nadu Open University had expressed a favourable attitude towards computer education. Their attitudes were differed in terms of sex, residence and the group of study.

Anuradha K. (2006) conducted a study of television viewing behaviour of adolescents—its impact on their Cadmic achievement. Television watching times of adolescents studying 8, 9 and 10th standard in Government schools in Triupathi town. Multi-stage random sampling technique is used. In the first stage, five government schools were selected randomly and children who have television in their homes were identified. In the next stage, 16 children were selected from each class (8 boys and 8 girls of five school) the mothers of the selected children also constituted the sample. Thus, the total sample was 48 students and 48 mothers. Television viewing behaviour of adolescents was collected from types of subjects namely adolescents and mothers by using two tools. The following conclusions can be drawn from the study. Adolescent boys and girls do not differ significantly in their television watching time. Television watching time of adolescents does not differ Significantly across the grade. Television watching time of adolescents does not differ secured more percentage of marks than those without cable connection. There was not much significant effect of amount of television watching on adolescent's academic achievement.

Sheela and Nagaraj Somalingappa Talawar (2002) conduct a study on "the relationship between knowledge of ICT and attitude to the inclusion of ICT in teacher education among teacher educators in terms of level of knowledge of ICT, length of experience, gender, type of intuition and subject of teaching. It was find that the level of knowledge was positively related, gender and subject of specialisation did not have any bearing.

Gnanadevan R. (2006) studied that Attitude of Teachers towards Educational innovations. The main aim of his study was to find the attitude of higher secondary school teachers towards Educational Innovations Scale had been administered to a random sample of 150 teachers working in higher secondary schools. The data was analysed by 't' test. In this study the attitude towards educational innovations of higher secondary school teachers was highly favourable. There was no significant difference among the teachers working in higher secondary schools with respect to sex, type of school, location of the school and subject taught.

Studies Conducted in Aboard

The investigator identified 10 studies conducted in Abroad. The abstract of the studies are arranged and presented chronologically below.

Feldman S. (1996) studied the FM broadcast radio and it sends music and voice, with higher than FM radio for the classroom situation. In frequency modulation, louder sounds at the microphone cause the transmitter frequency to fluctuate farther, the transmitter power stays constant. FM is transmitted in the Very High Frequency (VHF-30 MHz) radio spectrum. VHF radio waves act more like light, travelling in straight lines; hence the reception range is generally limited to about 50-100 miles. During unusual upper atmospheric conditions, FM signals are occasionally reelected back towards the Earth by the ionosphere, resulting in long distance FM reception. FM receivers are subject to the capture effect, which causes distance FM reception. FM receives the strongest signal when multiple signals appear on the same frequency. FM receivers are relatively immune to lighting and spark interference.

Pease A.V. (1976) investigated the FM sub carrier services are secondary signals transmitted piggyback" along with the main programme for the teaching purpose. Special receivers are required to utilise these services. Analog channels may contain alternative programming, such as redoing service for the blind, background music or stereo sound signals. In some extremely crowded metropolitan areas, the sub channel programme might be an alternate foreign language radio programme for various ethnic groups. Sub carriers can also transmit digital data, such as station identification, the current song's name, web address, or stock quotes. In some countries, FM radios automatically retune themselves to the same channels in a different district by using sub-bands.

Investigation of computer use in Los Angles conducted by *Porandolecht* (1983) suggest that teachers need to participate in computer literacy course, more software should be produced for educational use, a network of resource centers needs to be established to design, and disseminate pertinent information of software on the criteria for selecting computer systems should be undertaken.

Carnes R. (1985) say that studies written by experts in the field reflect the advantages of using computers as opposed to using computers, but research is needed on the most effective ways of using them. The only hypothesis, which yielded a significant difference, rates of learning. Result also revealed that students working in groups of 3 or 4 computer tutorials had significantly better rates of learning than students working alone, while no significant in achievement or retention were observed.

Micheal (1993) from West Virginia University compared the effectiveness of the delivery of an interactive CAI module to traditional lecture of lab derived interactive learning system. It was found out that learning of a conceptual predictive technological concept was more effective with interactive CAI.

Webster-Stratton and Colleagues (1994) have developed a videotape/group discussion programme for young children (three to eight years old) with conduct problem. The programme was based on many of the same learning principles described earlier. A standard package of videotaped programmes of modeled parenting skills has been developed. These videos contained 250 vignettes and about two minutes each included examples of parents interacting with their children in both appropriate ways. They were shown to groups of parents, and following each vignette there is a therapist-led discussion of the relevant interactions. Parents were also given homework assignments that allow them to practice skills at their children.

Micheal (1995) conducted an experimental study with to objectives to develop multimedia based modular for science on VII standard and to measure the effectiveness of multimedia based modular approach with special reference to low achievers. Two matched groups of achievers and normal group comprising average and above average students formed the sample for the study. The control and normal group was taught through multimedia based modular approach. The media method was more effective than the traditional lecture method in teaching of science and it enabled to low achievers to cope up with normal students to greater extent.

Lee (1996) says the at the technology use pattern of survey participants showed that Internet applications were the most highly used technology category with 78 per cent of respondents reporting use the Internet. However, only 30 per cent responded that they used internet for teaching purpose, Results indicated the familiarity with and knowledge of technology was the most important factors in explaining the differences among groups.

Martin (1997) pointed out in his findings this study examined the problem of financing of information Technology in higher education institutions, the results of the survey showed that respondents expect their use if the internet and the world wide web to increase in the next five years. With the use of client/server computing increasing at all institutions, and the rapid growth in the use of the Internet and the World Wide Web, the results of study should be valid to many other institutions.

Danilak Linda Fay (1999) investigated the effectiveness of multimedia instructional strategy in teaching science to slow learners. The study was undertaken with two objectives in view: (*i*) to developed multimedia package for class VIII science subject; and (*ii*) to measure the effectiveness of multimedia instructional strategy with special reference to slow learners. Two matched groups of slow learners were formed for the purpose of this experiment and normal group comprising average and above average students was also formed in order to assess how far multimedia instructional strategy enabled the slow learners to cope with normal students. The control group and the normal group were taught traditional lecture method while the experimental group was taught through multimedia instructional strategy. The obtained results showed that the multimedia instructional strategy was more effective than the traditional lecture methods in teaching science and it enabled the slow learners to cope with normal student to a considerable extent.

Forthcoming chapter deals with the methodology of the study.

Chapter 9

Methodology of the Study

INTRODUCTION

The present study is an experimental research aimed to measure the "Awareness on ICT's Among PG Teachers in Higher Secondary Schools" among the PG teachers of Tiruchirapalli district of Tamilnadu. The methodology followed in the present study is described in this chapter. The sample selected for this study was 200 PG teachers working in and around schools of Tiruchirapalli district in Tamilnadu. A questionnaire to measure the awareness on ICT's among PG Teachers with 51 items in four point scale with the various components of ICT's such as Computers, Internet, Edusat, e-mail and Online devices were considered. The questionnaire was administered among the above sample. Suitable statistical techniques were applied to analyse the data. The objectives of the study, the design of the study, size of the sample, development of the tool, statistical techniques used have been reported in the present study.

OBJECTIVES OF THE STUDY

The major objective of the study was to measure the Awareness on ICT's among PG Teachers in Higher Secondary Schools in total.

The specific objectives have been,

1. To find out the significant difference in the level of Awareness on ICT's among PG Teachers with respect to the Locality *i.e.,* Rural or Urban.
2. To find out the significant difference in the level of Awareness on ICT's among PG Teachers with respect to Sex *i.e.,* Male or Female.
3. To find out the significant difference in the level of Awareness on ICT's among PG Teachers with respect to Type of School *i.e.,* Girls school or Co-education schools.
4. To find out the significant difference in the level of Awareness on ICT's among PG Teachers with respect to the Type of Management *i.e.,* Government, Aided and Self-financing schools.
5. To find out the significant difference in the level of Awareness on ICT's among PG Teachers with respect to the Educational Qualification *i.e.,* PG with B.Ed, degree, PG with M.Ed, degree and PG with M.Phil. or Ph.D.
6. To find out the significant difference in the level of Awareness on ICT's among PG Teachers with respect to their previous knowledge in Computers whether they have or not.
7. To find out the significant relationship in the level of Awareness on ICT's in total between the various components of ICT's such as Computers, Internet, Edusat, e-mail and Online devices among themselves.

HYPOTHESES OF THE STUDY

The major hypotheses of the study were:

1. There is No Significant Difference in the level of Awareness on ICT's among PG Teachers in Higher Secondary Schools in total.

2. There is No Significant Difference in the level of Awareness on ICT's among PG Teachers in Higher Secondary Schools with respect to the Locality *i.e.*, Rural or Urban.
3. There is No Significant Difference in the level of Awareness on ICT's among PG Teachers in Higher Secondary Schools with respect to Sex *i.e.,* Male or Female.
4. There is No Significant Difference in the level of Awareness on ICT's among PG Teachers in Higher Secondary Schools with respect to the Type of School *i.e.,* Girls school or Co-education schools.
5. There is No Significant Difference in the level of Awareness on ICT's among PG Teachers in Higher Secondary Schools with respect to the Type of School Management *i.e.,* Government, Aided and Self-financing schools.
6. There is No Significant Difference in the level of Awareness on ICT's among PG Teachers in Higher Secondary Schools with respect to the Educational Qualification *i.e.,* PG with B.Ed, degree, PG with M.Ed, degree and PG with M.Phil. or Ph.D.
7. There is No Significant Difference in the level of Awareness on ICT's among PG Teachers in Higher Secondary Schools with respect to their previous knowledge in Computers whether they have or not.
8. There is No Significant Relationship in the level of Awareness on ICT's among PG Teachers in Higher Secondary Schools between the various components of ICT's such as Computers, Internet, Edusat, e-mail and Online devices among themselves.

DESIGN OF THE STUDY

The present study belongs to Normative Survey research. The design of the study is presented in the following schematic representation table:

Table 9.1. Schematic Representation of the Survey Design

S. No.	Type	Sources
1.	Nature of the Survey Research	Normative Survey Research study
2.	Variables	Locality, Sex, Type of School, Type of School Management, Educational Qualification and the Previous knowledge in computers whether they have or not.
3.	Tool used	Questionnaire to measure the awareness on ICT's among PG-Teachers.
4.	Sampling Technique	Random sampling Technique.
5.	Size of the sample	200 PG-Teachers working in 19 schools in and around Tiruchirapalli district of Tamilnadu.
6.	Statistical techniques used	Average, Standard deviation, 't' test and Correlation analysis

The table 9.1 shows that the nature of the study was Normative Survey Research study; the variables used in the survey were Locality *i.e.* Urban and Rural, Sex *i.e.* Male and Female, Type of School *i.e.,* Girls school or Co-Education schools, Type of School Management *i.e.,* Government, Aided and Self-financing schools, Educational Qualification *i.e.* PG with B.Ed, degree, PG with M.Ed, degree and PG with M.Phil. or Ph.D, and their previous knowledge in Computers whether they have or not. The tool used in the study was an Questionnaire developed to measure the Awareness on ICT's among the PG teachers with 51 items on four Point scale. The sample selected for this study was 200 PG teachers working in 19 schools in and around Tiruchirapalli district of Tamilnadu. The statistical techniques used in the study were Average, Standard deviation,'t' test and Correlation analysis.

DEFINITIONS OF KEY TERMS AND THEIR OPERATIONAL DEFINITION

The title of the study is: *"Awareness on ICT's Among PG Teachers in Higher Secondary Schools".* The key terms of the title are Awareness, ICT's, Higher Secondary Schools and PG Teachers whose operational definitions are defined.

Awareness : It means having knowledge of fact. It is the state of being aware of something. In the present study it refers to the degree of knowledge of P.G Teachers about ICT's.

ICT's : The Information Communication Technology's (ICT's) are not single technology, but combinations of hardware, software, media, and delivery systems. They differ in several important dimensions from older technologies: they can integrate multiple media into single educational applications; they are interactive and include the capacity to control, manipulate, and contribute to the information environment. They are flexible, offering freedom from rigid scheduling and barriers of time and location; through connectivity, they provide access to every other person on the planet who has an internet account, to hundreds of thousands of information archives, and to millions of web pages. These four dimensions such as integration of multi-media, interactivity, flexibility of use, and connectivity-distinguish digital ICTs from previous technologies.

C. Higher Secondary Schools : In the school educational system in Tamilnadu is divided into two types *viz.,* School Education and Collegiate Education. In the School Education, the schools are further divided as Primary schools where the students are taught from standard 1 to 5, Middle schools in which the students are taught from standard 1 to 8, High schools where the students are taught from standards 6 to 10 and Higher Secondary schools in which students were taught either from standards 6- 12 or standards 11 and 12 alone.

PG Teachers : The teachers handling the standards 11 and 12 of Higher Secondary schools are categorised as PG Teachers whose essential educational qualification is any PG degree with B.Ed., There may be PG teachers with higher qualifications such as PG degree with M.Ed. or M.Phil. or Ph.D. also.

SAMPLE SELECTION

The nature of the study was Normative Survey Research study. The sample selected for this study was 200 PG teachers

Table 9.2. Name and Number of the Sample Selected

S. No.	Name of the School	Nature of Management	Sex		Total
			M	F	
1.	R.C Hr.Sec.School	Aided	-	2	2
2.	G.H.S.S Kurumbalur	Govt	-	4	4
3.	G.H.S.S Esanai	Govt	2	3	5
4.	G.H.S.S Peralai	Govt	1	1	2
5.	G.H.S.S Keelapulur	Govt	3	1	4
6.	St.Jeosph Hr. Sec. School, Trichy	Aided	-	13	13
7.	G.H.S.S Viralimalai	Govt	5	2	7
8.	G.H.S.S Marungapuri	Govt	4	6	10
9.	Khaja Mian Hr.Sec.School	Aided	12	-	12
10.	Alpha Plus Matric Hr. Sec.School	Self-financing	7	16	23
11.	G.C.H.S.S	Aided	2	34	36
12.	Alaimagal H.S.S	Self-financing	1	10	11
13.	G.C.H.S.S Kovilpatti	Govt	7	9	16
14.	S.D.A Hr.S.S	Self-financing	7	19	26
15.	British Matric Hr.S.S	Self-financing	2	2	4
16.	C.S.I Mahimaipuram	Aided	3	2	5
17.	G.H.S.S Ayyampettai	Govt	4	5	9
18.	G.H.S.S Manaparai	Govt	4	5	9
19.	Rover Hr.S.S	Self-financing	-	1	1
	Total		67	133	200

working in 19 schools in and around Tiruchirapalli district of Tamilnadu. The number of samples and the schools from which the samples are selected are given in the table 9.2.

TOOL DEVELOPMENT

As a standard tool was not available to measure the Awareness on ICT's among PG Teachers in Higher Secondary Schools, the investigator happened to prepared an Questionnaire to measure the Awareness on ICT's. The investigator went on developing suitable items. The investigator prepared the items with four options such as Strongly Agree, Agree, and Disagree and Strongly Disagree. While preparing the items, the investigator dealt with significant ideas and gave attention to the items uniformly selected from the various components of ICT's such as Computers, Internet, Edusat, e-mail and Online devices. The investigator herself satisfied after the deletion, addition and modification of the items prepared. It was shown to two PG Computer teachers and two teacher educators for verifying the suitability of the items.

There were 76 items in the various components on ICT's. The number of items selected from five various components on ICT's are given in the table 9.3 preliminary draft of the questionnaire.

Table 9.3

S. No.	Objective	No. of items
1.	Computers	17
2.	Internet	14
3.	Edusat	13
4.	e-mail	16
5.	Online devices	16
	Total	**76**

Preliminary Draft of the Questionnaire

After preparing the preliminary draft of the questionnaires the investigator gave it to the PG Computer teachers and two teacher educators. They critically analysed the items and gave their suggestions. Afterwards the investigator changed some of the items and then modified.

The preliminary draft was neatly typed and administered on the selected PG teachers. The 30 PG teachers were selected as sample for the pilot study and the test was conducted. The teachers took around 45 minutes to complete the test item. The questionnaire was scored and arranged in order from the highest to the lowest. The 28% (8) of the questionnaire were selected from the highest score and 28% (8) were selected from the lower score. The middle score 44% were kept aside. The number of correct response in each item for both high scoring and low scoring groups were completed. The level of difficulty value was determined by applying appropriate formula namely R/N x 100 where R refers to the total number of items answered correctly and N refers to the total number of Teachers attempted to answer the test items. To determine the discriminative index the formula RHi – RLo/N was applied where RHi refers to the number of Teachers in the higher group who answered the test item correctly "RLo" refers to the number of Teachers in the home group who answered the test item correctly and N-refers to the number of Teachers.

Table 9.4. Final Draft of the Questionnaire

S. No.	Objective	No. of items
1.	Computers	11
2.	Internet	10
3.	Edusat	8
4.	E-mail	12
5.	Online devices	10
	Total	**51**

After calculating the values for each item it was found that 14 and 11 items were not having adequate scores of difficulty value and discriminatory index. The total number of 76 items was reduced to 51 items for the final study. The 51 items selected for the present study is presented in table 9.4.

ADMINISTERING THE TOOL

The tool was administered among the 200 PG teachers working in 19 schools in and around Tiruchirapalli district of Tamilnadu randomly. The details of the sample in the study are discussed under the sample selection. The investigator instructed to read all the items carefully and put the tick mark near the appropriate options. Afterwards the investigator collected the filled in questionnaire.

STATISTICAL MEASURES USED IN THE STUDY

After collecting the filled in questionnaire the investigator scored all the questionnaires. Master table was prepared by plotting the scores. Different statistical measures were used in the study. Mean, Standard deviation, 't' values were calculated to find out the significant difference between the two variables and correlation were found to find out the significant relationship between the various factors in ICT's. The investigator rejected or accepted the hypotheses based on the 't' and 'r' values.

LIMITATIONS

1. The questionnaire has included only five components of ICT's such as Computers, Internet, Edusat, e-mail and Online devices for want of time.

2. The investigator limited the variables used in the study as Locality, Sex, Type of School, Type of School Management, Educational Qualification and the Previous knowledge in computers whether they have or not.

3. The investigator confined his study with 200 PG teachers as samples with limited time.

4. The investigator found a limited research studies, journals on the selected topics on ICT's.

5. The investigator conducted the study only among the Higher secondary schools that too among the PG teachers alone.

The forth coming Chapter deals with the Data Analysis.

Data Analysis

Chapter 10

INTRODUCTION

The collected data as discussed in the previous Chapter were subjected to different types of analysis. Different Statistical techniques such as Mean, Standard Deviation,'t' test and Correlation were found. The results are presented in this Chapter along with the interpretations rationally. The results are presented in eight classifications such as the level of awareness on ICT devices with respect to Sex of the PG teachers *i.e.* Male and Female, Locality of the PG teachers *i.e.* Urban and Rural, Type of the School *i.e.* Girls and Co-Education schools, Type of Management *i.e.* Government, Aided and Self-financing, Educational Qualification of the teachers i.e. P.G B.Ed., P.G.M.Ed., and PG M.Phil. Previous Knowledge in Computers *i.e.* Yes and No and finally the subjects taught by the teachers *i.e.* Arts and Science and finally the level of relationship between the various ICT devices among themselves in total. The further classifications such as the awareness on Computers, Internet, Edusat, e-mail and Online devices were also considered.

Section A : Level of Awareness on ICT Devices among, the PG Teachers with Respect to Sex

This section deals with the analysis of the mean scores on the Awareness of ICT among the PG teachers in total with

respect to Sex *i.e.* Male and Female. It also deals with the analysis of the mean scores on the Awareness of the PG teachers towards the various components of ICT such as Computers, Internet, Edusat, e-mail and Online devices.

Section B : Level of Awareness on ICT Devices among the PG Teachers with Respect to Locality

This section deals with the analysis of the mean scores on the Awareness of ICT among the PG teachers in total with respect to Locality *i.e.* Urban and Rural. It also deals with the analysis of the mean scores on the Awareness of the PG teachers towards the various components of ICT such as Computers, Internet, Edusat, E-mail and Online devices.

Section C : Level of Awareness on ICT Devices among the PG Teachers with Respect to Type of the School

This section deals with the analysis of the mean scores on the Awareness of ICT among the PG teachers in total with respect to Type of the School *i.e.* Girls School and Co-Education Schools. It also deals with the analysis of the mean scores on the Awareness of the PG teachers towards the various components of ICT such as Computers, Internet, Edusat, E-mail and Online devices.

Section D : Level of Awareness on ICT Devices among the PG Teachers with Respect to Management of the Schools

This section deals with the analysis of the mean scores on the Awareness of ICT among the PG teachers in total with respect to Management of the School i.e. Government, Aided and Self-financing Schools. It also deals with the analysis of the mean scores on the Awareness of the PG teachers towards the various components of ICT such as Computers, Internet, Edusat, E-mail and Online devices.

Section E : Level of Awareness on ICT Devices among the PG Teachers with Respect to Qualification

This section deals with the analysis of the mean scores on the Awareness of ICT among the PG teachers in total with

respect to Qualification of the PG teachers i.e. P.G B.Ed., P.G.M.Ed., and PG M.Phil. It also deals with the analysis of the mean scores on the Awareness of the PG teachers towards the various components of ICT such as Computers, Internet, Edusat, E-mail and Online devices.

Section F : Level of Awareness on ICT Devices among the PG Teachers with Respect to Knowledge in Computers

This section deals with the analysis of the mean scores on the Awareness of ICT among the PG teachers in total with respect to their Previous knowledge in computers *i.e.* Yes or No. It also deals with the analysis of the mean scores on the Awareness of the PG teachers towards the various components of ICT such as Computers, Internet, Edusat, E-mail and Online devices.

Section G : Level of Awareness on ICT Devices among the PG Teachers with Respect to Subjects Taught by the Teachers

This section deals with the analysis of the mean scores on the Awareness of ICT among the PG teachers in total with respect to the Subjects taught by the PG teachers *i.e.* Arts and Science. It also deals with the analysis of the mean scores on the Awareness of the PG teachers towards the various components of ICT such as Computers, Internet, Edusat, E-mail and Online devices. The results are presented in the following tables 10.21 to 10.22.

Section H : Significant Relationship in Awareness on ICT Devices among the PG Teachers

This section deals with the Correlation analysis of the mean scores on the Awareness of ICT among the PG teachers in total between the various components of ICT such as Computers, Internet, Edusat, E-mail and Online devices among themselves.

Section A : Level of Awareness on ICT Devices among the PG Teachers with Respect to Sex

This section deals with the analysis of the mean scores on the Awareness of ICT among the PG teachers in total with

respect to Sex *i.e.* Male and Female. It also deals with the analysis of the mean scores on the Awareness of the PG teachers towards the various components of ICT such as Computers, Internet, Edusat, e-mail and Online devices. The results are presented in the following tables 10.1 and 10.2.

Table 10.1. Significantly Difference in the Mean Scores of the Awareness on ICT Devices in Total with Respect to Sex of the PG Teachers

S. No.	Category		N	Mean	SD	't' Value		Remarks
						Cal	Table	
1.	ICT's in	M	67	69.84	7.54	0.03	1.96	NSD
	Total	F	133	69.81	7.15			

From the above table 10.1 it is seen that the't' value 0.03 of the mean scores of the awareness on ICT in total with respect to Sex is Not Significantly Different at 0.05 level. Hence the framed null hypothesis that there is no difference in the awareness on ICT in total with respect to Sex is accepted.

Table 10.2. Significant Difference in the Mean Score of Awareness on the Various ICT Devices with Respect to Sex of the PG Teachers

S. No.	Category		N	Mean	SD	't' Value		Remarks
						Cal	Table	
1.	Computers	M	67	71.87	8.55	1.15	1.96	NSD
		F	133	70.33	9.58			
2.	Internet	M	67	69.07	11.00	1.32	1.96	NSD
		F	133	67.07	9.66			
3.	Edusat	M	67	70.93	10.99	0.69	1.96	NSD
		F	133	69.75	12.10			
4.	e-mail	M	67	68.84	8.42	2.65	1.96	SD
		F	133	72.56	11.00			
5.	Online	M	67	69.28	9.00	0.50	1.96	NSD
		F	133	69.98	10.24			

It is seen from the above table 10.2 that the't' values 1.15, 1.32, 0.69 and 0.50 between mean values of Awareness on ICT devices among the Male and Female teachers pertaining to Computers, Internet, Edusat and On Line devices are Not Significantly Different and 2.65 of the e-mail is Significantly Different at 0.05 level. Hence the framed Null hypotheses that there is no difference in the mean scores of teachers PG B.Ed. and PG M.Ed. pertaining to Computers, Internet, Edusat and On Line devices were accepted and is rejected among e-mail alone.

Section B : Level of Awareness on ICT Devices among the PG Teachers with Respect to Locality

This section deals with the analysis of the mean scores on the Awareness of ICT among the PG teachers in total with respect to Locality *i.e.* Urban and Rural. It also deals with the analysis of the mean scores on the Awareness of the PG teachers towards the various components of ICT such as Computers, Internet, Edusat, e-mail and Online devices. The results are presented in the following tables 10.3 and 10.4.

Table 10.3. Significantly Difference in the Mean Score of the Awareness on ICT Devices in Total with Respect to Locality of the Teachers

S. No.	Category		N	Mean	SD	't' Value		Re-marks
						Cal	Table	
1.	ICT's in Total	U	130	70.38	7.74	1.60	1.96	NSD
		R	70	68.77	6.20			

On observing the above table 10.3 it is clearly seen that the't' value 1.60 of the mean scores of the awareness on ICT in total with respect to Locality of the teachers is Not Significantly Different at 0.05 level. Hence the framed null hypothesis that there is no difference in the awareness on ICT in total with respect to Locality of the teachers is accepted.

Table 10.4. Significant Difference in the Mean Scores of Awareness on the Various ICT Devices with Respect to Locality of the Teachers

S. No.	Category		N	Mean	SD	't' Value		Remarks
						Cal	Table	
1.	Computers	U	130	70.63	10.14	0.49	1.96	NSD
		R	70	71.24	7.37			
2.	Internet	U	130	68.08	10.41	0.66	1.96	NSD
		R	70	67.11	9.67			
3.	Edusat	U	130	69.81	12.49	0.59	1.96	NSD
		R	70	70.77	10.21			
4.	e-mail	U	130	72.77	10.61	2.87	1.96	SD
		R	70	68.61	9.31			
5.	Online	U	130	71.12	10.56	3.47	1.96	SD
		R	70	66.64	7.52			

From the above table 10.4 it is understood that the 't' values 0.49, 0.66 and 0.59 between mean values of Awareness on ICT devices among the Urban and Rural school teachers pertaining to Computers, Internet and Edusat are Not Significantly Different and 2.87 and 3.47 of the e-mail and Online devices is significantly different at 0.05 level. Hence the framed Null hypotheses that there is no difference in the mean scores of urban and rural school teachers pertaining to computers, Internet and Edusat were accepted and are rejected among e-mail and Online devices.

Section C : Level of Awareness on ICT Devices among the PG Teachers with Respect to Type of the School

This section deals with the analysis of the mean scores on the Awareness of ICT among the PG teachers in total with respect to Type of the School *i.e.* Girls School and Co-education Schools. It also deals with the analysis of the mean scores on the Awareness of the PG teachers towards the various components of ICT such as Computers, Internet, Edusat, e-mail and Online devices. The results are presented in the following tables 10.5 and 10.6.

Table 10.5. Significantly Difference in the Mean Scores of the Awareness on ICT Devices in Total with Respect to Type of school

S. No.	Category		N	Mean	SD	't' Value		Re-marks
						Cal	Table	
1.	ICT's in	Girls	50	71.04	6.42	1.49	1.96	NSD
	Total	Co-Edn	150	69.41	7.50			

It is clearly seen from the above table 10.5 that the 't' value 1.49 of the mean scores of the awareness on ICT in total between the teachers of Girls and Co-education school is Not Significantly Different at 0.05 level. Hence the framed null hypothesis that there is no difference in the awareness on ICT in total between the teachers of Girls and Co-education school is accepted.

Table 10.6. Significant Difference in the Mean Scores of Awareness on the Various ICT Devices with Respect to Type of School

S. No.	Category		N	Mean	SD	't' Value		Rem-arks
						Cal	Table	
1.	Computers	Girls	50	68.94	9.28	1.69	1.96	NSD
		Co-Edn	150	71.48	9.19			
2.	Internet	Girls	50	64.62	9.31	2.67	1.96	SD
		Co-Edn	150	68.78	10.23			
3.	Edusat	Girls	50	70.64	11.49	0.35	1.96	NSD
		Co-Edn	150	69.98	11.84			
4.	E-mail	Girls	50	78.16	9.85	5.84	1.96	SD
		Co-Edn	150	69.03	9.48			
5.	Online	Girls	50	73.48	9.97	3.35	1.96	SD
		Co-Edn	150	68.24	9.45			

From the above table 10.4 it is clear that the 't' values 1.69, 0.35 and 0.59 between mean values of Awareness on ICT devices among the teachers working in Girls School and Co- education schools pertaining to Computers and Edusat are Not Significantly Different and 2.67, 5.84 and 3.35 of the Internet, e-mail and Online devices is Significantly Different at 0.05 level. Hence the framed Null hypotheses that there is no difference in the mean scores of teachers working in Girls School and Co-education schools pertaining to Computers and Edusat were accepted and are rejected among Internet, e-mail and Online devices.

Section D : Level of Awareness on ICT Devices among the PG Teachers with Respect to Management of the Schools

This section deals with the analysis of the mean scores on the Awareness of ICT among the PG teachers in total with respect to Management of the School *i.e.* Government, Aided and Self-financing Schools. It also deals with the analysis of the mean scores on the Awareness of the PG teachers towards the various components of ICT such as Computers, Internet, Edusat, e-mail and Online devices. The results are presented in the following tables 10.7 and 10.12.

Table 10.7. Significantly Difference in the Mean Scores of the Awareness on ICT Devices in Total between Government and Aided School PG Teachers

S. No.	Category		N	Mean	SD	't' Value		Re-marks
						Cal	Table	
1.	ICT's in	Govt.	70	68.83	6.19	1.08	1.96	NSD
	Total	Aided	68	70.03	6.91			

From the above table 10.7 it is obviously seen that the 't' value 1.08 of the mean scores of the awareness on ICT in total between the Government and Aided school teachers is Not Significantly Different at 0.05 level. Hence the framed null hypothesis that there is no difference in the awareness on ICT in total between the Government and Aided school teachers is accepted.

Table 10.8. Significant difference in the Mean Scores of Awareness on the Various ICT Devices between Government and Aided School PG Teachers

S. No.	Category		N	Mean	SD	't' Value		Remarks
						Cal	Table	
1.	Computers	Govt.	70	70.74	7.59	0.84	1.96	NSD
		Aided	68	69.52	9.34			
2.	Internet	Govt.	70	67.17	8.87	0.85	1.96	NSD
		Aided	68	65.76	10.48			
3.	Edusat	Govt.	70	70.07	10.27	0.31	1.96	NSD
		Aided	68	69.49	11.92			
4.	e-mail	Govt.	70	69.20	8.92	2.86	1.96	SD
		Aided	68	74.13	11.26			
5.	Online	Govt.	70	67.47	8.93	2.54	1.96	SD
		Aided	68	71.44	9.43			

It is obviously seen from the above table 10.8 that the 't' values 0.84, 0.85 and 0.31 between mean values of Awareness on ICT devices among the Government and Aided school teachers pertaining to Computers, Internet and Edusat are Not Significantly Different and 2.86 and 2.54 of the e-mail and Online devices is Significantly Different at 0.05

Table 10.9. Significantly Difference in the Mean Scores of the Awareness on ICT Devices in Total between Aided and Self-financing School PG Teachers

S. No.	Category		N	Mean	SD	't' Value		Remarks
						Cal	Table	
1.	ICT's in	Aided	68	70.03	6.91	0.50	1.96	NSD
	Total	Self-Fin	62	70.71	8.60			

level. Hence the framed Null hypotheses that there is no difference in the mean scores of Government and Aided school teachers pertaining to Computers, Internet and Edusat were accepted and are rejected among e-mail and Online devices.

From the above table 10.9 it is clear that the 't' value 0.50 of the mean scores of the awareness on ICT in total between the Aided and Self-financing school teachers is Not Significantly Different at 0.05 level. Hence the framed null hypothesis that there is no difference in the awareness on ICT in total between the Aided and Self-financing school teachers is accepted.

Table 4.10. Significant Difference in the Mean Scores of Awareness of the Various ICT Devices between Aided and Self-financing School Teachers

S. No.	Category		N	Mean	SD	't' Value		Rem-arks
						Cal	Table	
1.	Computers	Aided	68	69.52	9.34	1.52	1.96	NSD
		Self-fin	62	72.19	10.73			
2.	Internet	Aided	68	65.76	10.48	2.58	1.96	SD
		Self-fin	62	70.55	10.65			
3.	Edusat	Aided	68	69.49	11.92	0.66	1.96	NSD
		Self-fin	62	70.95	13.12			
4.	e-mail	Aided	68	74.13	11.26	1.87	1.96	NSD
		Self-fin	62	70.61	10.25			
5.	Online	Aided	68	71.44	9.43	0.91	1.96	NSD
		Self-fin	62	69.82	10.85			

It is understood from the above table 10.10 that the 't' values 1.52, 0.66, 1.87 and 0.91 between mean values of Awareness on ICT devices among the teachers working in Aided and Self-financing schools pertaining to Computers, Edusat, e-mail and Online devices are Not Significantly Different and 2.58 of the Internet, is Significantly Different at 0.05 level. Hence the framed Null hypotheses that there is no difference in the mean scores of teachers working in

Aided and Self-financing schools pertaining to Computers, Edusat and Online devices were accepted and is rejected among Internet and e-mail.

Table 4.11. Significantly Differences in the Mean Scores of the Awareness on ICT Devices in Total between Government and Self-financing School Teachers

S. No.	Category		N	Mean	SD	't' Value		Remarks
						Cal	Table	
1.	ICT's in Total	Govt.	70	68.83	6.19	1.45	1.96	NSD
		Self-fin	62	70.71	8.60			

From the above table 10.11 it is clearly seen that the 't' value 1.45 of the mean scores of the awareness on ICT in total between the Government and Self-financing school teachers is Not Significantly Different at 0.05 level. Hence the framed null hypothesis that there is no difference in the awareness on ICT in total between the Government and Self-financing school teachers is accepted.

Table 10.12. Significant Difference in the Mean Scores of Awareness on the Various ICT Devices between Government and Self-financing School Teachers

S. No.	Category		N	Mean	SD	't' Value		Remarks
						Cal	Table	
1.	Computers	Govt.	70	70.74	7.59	0.90	1.96	NSD
		Self-fin	62	72.19	10.73			
2.	Internet	Govt.	70	67.17	8.87	1.99	1.96	SD
		Self-fin	62	70.55	10.65			
3.	Edusat	Govt.	70	70.07	10.27	0.43	1.96	NSD
		Self-fin	62	70.95	13.12			
4.	e-mail	Govt.	70	69.20	8.92	0.85	1.96	NSD
		Self-fin	62	70.61	10.25			
5.	Online	Govt.	70	67.47	8.93	1.36	1.96	NSD
		Self-fin	62	69.82	10.85			

On observing the above table 10.12 it is understood that the 't' values 0.90, 0.43, 0.85 and 1.36 between mean values of Awareness on ICT devices among the teachers working in Government and Self-Financing schools pertaining to Computers, Edusat, e-mail and Online devices are Not Significantly Different and 1.99 of the Internet is Significantly Different at 0.05 level. Hence the framed Null hypotheses that there is no difference in the mean scores of teachers working in Government and Self-Financing schools pertaining to Computers, Edusat and Online devices were accepted and is rejected among Internet and e-mail.

Section E : Level of Awareness on ICT Devices among the PG Teachers with Respect to Qualification

This section deals with the analysis of the mean scores on the Awareness of ICT among the PG teachers in total with respect to Qualification of the PG teachers *i.e.* P.G B.Ed., P.G.M.Ed., and PG M.Phil. It also deals with the analysis of the mean scores on the Awareness of the PG teachers towards the various components of ICT such as Computers, Internet, Edusat, e-mail and Online devices. The results are presented in the following tables 10.13 to 10.18.

Table 10.13. Significant Difference in the Mean Scores of the Awareness on ICT Devices in Total between the PG Teachers whose Qualifications are PG B.Ed. and PG M.Ed.

S. No.	Category		N	Mean	SD	't' Value		Remarks
						Cal	Table	
1.	ICT's in Total	PG B.Ed.	122	69.71	6.96	0.34	1.96	NSD
		PG M.Ed.	35	70.17	7.39			

From the above table 10.13 it is obvious that the 't' value 0.34 of the mean scores of the awareness on ICT in total between the PG teachers whose qualifications are PG B.Ed. and PG M.Ed. is Not Significantly Different at 0.05 level. Hence the framed null hypothesis that there is no difference in the awareness on ICT in total between the PG teachers whose qualifications are PG B.Ed. and PG M.Ed. is accepted.

Table 10.14. Significant Difference in the Mean Scores of Awareness on the Various ICT Devices between the PG Teachers whose Qualifications are PG B.Ed. and PG M.Ed.

S. No.	Category		N	Mean	SD	't' Value		Remarks
						Cal	Table	
1.	Computers	PG B.Ed.	122	70.61	8.98	0.60	1.96	NSD
		PG M.Ed.	35	69.57	9.48			
2.	Internet	PG B.Ed.	122	67.11	9.99	0.03	1.96	NSD
		PG M.Ed.	35	67.17	9.00			
3.	Edusat	PG B.Ed.	122	69.81	12.09	0.65	1.96	NSD
		PG M.Ed.	35	71.20	10.79			
4.	e-mail	PG B.Ed.	122	72.06	9.38	0.39	1.96	NSD
		PG M.Ed.	35	72.80	11.59			
5.	Online	PG B.Ed.	122	69.52	9.89	0.54	1.96	NSD
		PG M.Ed.	35	70.49	9.16			

From the above table 10.14 it is observed that the 't' values 0.60, 0.03, 0.65, 0.39 and 0.54 between mean values of Awareness on ICT devices among the teachers with qualification PG B.Ed. and PG M.Ed. pertaining to Computers, Internet, Edusat, e-mail and Online devices are Not Significantly Different at 0.05 level. Hence the framed Null hypothesis that there is no difference in the mean scores of teachers PG B.Ed. and PG M.Ed. pertaining to Computers, Internet, Edusat, e-mail and On Line devices were accepted.

Table 4.15. Significantly Difference in the Mean Scores of the Awaareness on ICT Devices in Total between the PG Teachers whose Qualifications are PG M.Ed. and P.G. M.Phil.

S. No.	Category		N	Mean	SD	't' Value		Remarks
						Cal	Table	
1.	ICT' in	PG M.Ed.	35	70.17	7.39	0.19	1.96	NSD
	Total	PG M.Phil.	43	69.84	8.13			

From the above table 10.15 it is obviously understood that the't' value 0.19 of the mean scores of the awareness on ICT in total between the PG teachers whose qualifications are PG M.Ed. and PG M.Phil. is Not Significantly Different at 0.05 level. Hence the framed null hypothesis that there is no difference in the awareness on ICT in total between the PG teachers whose qualifications is PG M.Ed. and PG M.Phil. is accepted.

Table 4.16. Significant Difference in the Mean Scores of Awareness on the Various ICT Devices between the PG Teachers whose Qualifications are PG M.Ed. and PG M.Phil.

S. No.	Category		N	Mean	SD	't' Value		Remarks
						Cal	Table	
1.	Computers	PG M.Ed.	35	69.57	9.48	1.36	1.96	NSD
		PG M.Phil.	43	72.56	9.80			
2.	Internet	PG M.Ed.	35	67.17	9.00	1.23	1.96	NSD
		PG M.Phil.	43	70.00	11.31			
3.	Edusat	PG M.Ed.	35	71.20	10.79	0.38	1.96	NSD
		PG M.Phil.	43	70.23	11.60			
4.	e-mail	PG M.Ed.	35	72.80	11.59	1.84	1.96	NSD
		PG M.Phil.	43	68.00	11.39			
5.	Online	PG M.Ed.	35	70.49	9.16	0.73	1.96	NSD
		PG M.Phil.	43	68.88	10.30			

It is observed from the above table 10.16 that the 't' values 0.36, 1.23, 0.38, 1.84 and 0.73 between mean values of Awareness on ICT devices among the teachers with qualification PG M.Ed. and PG M.Phil. pertaining to Computers, Internet, Edusat, e-mail and Online devices are Not Significantly Different at 0.05 level. Hence the framed Null hypothesis that there is no difference in the mean scores of teachers PG M. Ed. and PG M. Phil. Pertaining to Computers, Internet, Edusat, e-mail and Online devices were accepted.

Table 10.17. Significantly Difference in the Mean Scores of the Awareness on ICT Devices in Total between the PG Teachers whose Qualifications are PG M.Ed. and PG M.Phil

S. No.	Category		N	Mean	SD	't' Value Cal	't' Value Table	Remarks
1.	ICT's in Total	PG B.Ed.	122	69.71	6.96	0.10	1.96	NSD
		PG M.Phil.	43	69.84	8.13			

From the above table 10.17 it is seen that the 't' value 0.10 of the mean scores of the awareness on ICT in total between the PG teachers whose qualifications are PG B.Ed. and PG M.Phil. is Not Significantly Different at 0.05 level. Hence the framed null hypothesis that there is no difference in the awareness on ICT in total between the PG teachers whose qualifications is PG B.Ed. and PG M.Phil. is accepted.

Table 10.18. Significant Difference in the Mean Scores of Awareness of the Various ICT Devices between the PG Teachers whose Qualifications are PG B.Ed. and PG M.Phil.

S. No.	Category		N	Mean	SD	't' Value Cal	't' Value Table	Remarks
1.	Computers	PG B.Ed.	122	70.61	8.98	1.20	1.96	NSD
		PG M.Phil.	43	72.56	9.80			
2.	Internet	PG B.Ed.	122	67.11	9.99	1.57	1.96	NSD
		PG M.Phil.	43	70.00	11.31			
3.	Edusat	PG B.Ed.	122	69.81	12.09	0.20	1.96	NSD
		PG M.Phil.	43	70.23	11.60			
4.	e-mail	PG B.Ed.	122	72.06	9.38	2.30	1.96	SD
		PG M.Phil.	43	68.00	11.39			
5.	Online	PG B.Ed.	122	69.52	9.89	0.36	1.96	NSD
		PG M.Phil.	43	66.88	10.30			

It is understood from the above table 10.18 that the 't' values 1.20, 1.57, 0.20 and 0.36 between mean values of Awareness on ICT devices among the teachers whose qualifications are PG B.Ed. and PG M.Phil. Pertaining to Computers, Internet, Edusat, and Online devices are Not Significantly Different and 2.30 of the e-mail is Significantly Different at 0.05 level. Hence the framed Null hypotheses that there is no difference in the mean scores of teachers whose qualifications are PG B.Ed. and PG M.Phil. Pertaining to Computers, Internet, Edusat, and Online devices were accepted and are rejected among e-mail.

Section F : Level of Awareness ICT Devices among the PG Teachers with Respect to Knowledge in Computers

This section deals with the analysis of the mean scores on the Awareness of ICT among the PG teachers in total with respect to their Previous knowledge in computers *i.e.* Yes or No. It also deals with the analysis of the mean scores on the Awareness of the PG teachers towards the various components of ICT such as Computers, Internet, Edusat, e-mail and Online devices. The results are presented in the following tables 10.19 to 10.20.

Table 4.19. Significantly Differences in the Mean Scores of the Awareness on ICT Devices in Total with Respect to Knowledge in Computers

S. No.	Category		N	Mean	SD	't' Value Cal	't' Value Table	Remarks
1.	ICT's in Total	Yes	145	70.99	7.35	4.14	1.96	SD
		No	55	66.75	6.10			

From the above table 10.19 it is seen that the 't' value 4.14 of the mean scores of the awareness on ICT in total between the PG teachers those who have and do not have computer knowledge is Significantly Different at 0.05 level. Hence the framed null hypothesis that there is no difference in the awareness on ICT in total between the PG teachers those who have and do not have computer knowledge is rejected.

Table 4.20. Significant Difference in the Mean Scores of Awareness on the Various ICT Devices with Respect to Knowledge in Computers

S. No.	Category		N	Mean	SD	't' Value		Remarks
						Cal	Table	
1.	Computers	Yes	145	72.62	8.95	4.75	1.96	SD
		No	55	66.16	8.44			
2.	Internet	Yes	145	69.74	10.26	5.40	1.96	SD
		No	55	62.47	7.72			
3.	Edusat	Yes	145	70.99	11.60	1.65	1.96	NSD
		No	55	67.93	11.88			
4.	e-mail	Yes	145	71.89	10.57	1.33	1.96	NSD
		No	55	69.80	9.64			
5.	Online	Yes	145	70.27	10.12	1.80	1.96	NSD
		No	55	67.65	8.80			

From the above table 10.20 it is understood that the 't' values 1.65, 1.33, and 1.80 between mean values of Awareness on ICT devices among the teachers those who have and do not have computer knowledge pertaining to Edusat, e-mail and Online devices are Not Significantly Different and 4.75 and 5.40 of the Computers and Internet is Significantly Different at 0.05 level. Hence the framed Null hypothesis that there is no difference in the mean scores of teachers those who have and do not have computer knowledge pertaining to Edusat, e-mail and Online devices were accepted and is rejected among Computers and Internet.

Section G : Level of Awareness on ICT Devices among the PG Teachers with Respect to Subjects Taught by the Teachers

This section deals with the analysis of the mean scores on the Awareness of ICT among the PG teachers in total with

respect to the Subjects taught by the PG teachers *i.e.* Arts and Science. It also deals with the analysis of the mean scores on the Awareness of the PG teachers towards the various components of ICT such as Computers, Internet, Edusat, e-mail and Online devices. The results are presented in the following tables 10.21 to 10.22.

Table 4.21. Significantly Difference in the Mean Scores of the Awareness on ICT Devices in Total with Respect to Subjects Taught by the Teachers

S. No.	Category		N	Mean	SD	't' Value		Remarks
						Cal	Table	
1.	ICT's in Total	Arts	89	69.78	7.95	0.08	1.96	NSD
		Science	111	69.86	6.71			

Table 4.22. Significant Difference in the Mean Scores of Awareness on the Various ICT Devices with Respect to Subjects Taught by the Teachers

S. No.	Category		N	Mean	SD	't' Value		Remarks
						Cal	Table	
1.	Computers	Arts	89	70.58	9.37	0.36	1.96	NSD
		Science	111	71.05	9.20			
2.	Internet	Arts	89	66.36	10.70	1.73	1.96	NSD
		Science	111	68.85	9.59			
3.	Edusat	Arts	89	71.08	12.28	1.01	1.96	NSD
		Science	111	69.40	11.26			
4.	e-mail	Arts	89	71.02	11.44	0.36	1.96	NSD
		Science	111	71.55	9.41			
5.	Online	Arts	89	70.21	9.73	0.85	1.96	NSD
		Science	111	69.02	9.90			

It is obviously seen from the table 10.21 that the 't' value 0.08 of the mean scores of the awareness on ICT in total between the PG teachers those who are teaching Arts and Science subjects is Not Significantly Different at 0.05 level. Hence the framed null hypothesis that there is no difference in the awareness on ICT in total between the PG teachers those who are teaching Arts and Science subjects is accepted.

From the table 10.22 it is clearly seen that the 't' values 0.36, 1.73, 1.01, 0.36 and 0.85 between mean values of Awareness on ICT devices among the Arts and Science teaching teachers pertaining to Computers, Internet, Edusat, e-mail and Online devices are Not Significantly Different at 0.05 level. Hence the framed Null hypotheses that there is no difference in the mean scores of Arts and Science teaching teachers pertaining to Computers, Internet, Edusat, e-mail and Online devices were accepted.

Section H : Significant Relationship in Awareness on ICT Devices among the PG Teachers

This section deals with the Correlation analysis of the mean scores on the Awareness of ICT among the PG teachers in total between the various components of ICT such as Computers, Internet, Edusat, e-mail and Online devices among themselves. The results are presented in the following tables 10.23 to 10.27.

Table 10.23. Significant Relationship in the Mean Scores of Awareness between Computers and the Other Components of ICT Devices

S.No.	Category	N	't' Value	Remarks
1.	Computer-Internet	200	0.4815	SC
2.	Computer-Edusat	200	0.4300	SC
3.	Computer-e-mail	200	0.1758	NSC
4.	Computer-Online	200	0.2468	NSC

On observing the table 10.23 it is understood that the 't' values 0.1758 and 0.2468 between the mean values of awareness on Computer and e-mail and Computer and Online are Not Significantly Correlated and 0.4815 and 0.4300 between Computer and Internet and Computer and Edusat are Significantly Correlated at 0.05 level. Hence the framed Null hypothesis that there is no relationship between the Edusat and the other devices is accepted except Computer and Internet and Computer and Edusat.

Table 10.24. Significant Realtionship in the Mean Scores of Awareness between Internet and the other ICT Devices

S.No.	Category	N	't' Value	Remarks
1.	Internet-Computer	200	0.4815	SC
2.	Internet –Edusat	200	0.4599	SC
3.	Internet- e-mail	200	0.2238	NSC
4.	Internet- Online	200	0.3356	NSC

On observing the table 10.24 it is seen that the 't' value 0.2238 and 0.3356 between the mean values of awareness on Internet and e-mail and Internet and Online are Not Significantly Correlated and 0.4815 and 0.4599 between Internet and Computer and Internet and Edusat are Significantly Correlated at 0.05 level. Hence the framed Null hypothesis that there is no relationship between the Edusat and the other devices is accepted except Internet and Computer and Internet and Edusat.

Table 4.25. Significant Relationship in the Mean Scores of Awareness between Edusat and the Other ICT Devices

S.No.	Category	N	't' Value	Remarks
1.	Edusat- Computer	200	0.4300	SC
2.	Edusat- Internet	200	0.4599	SC
3.	Edusat - e-mail	200	0.3481	NSC
4.	Edusat - Online	200	0.4799	SC

On observing the table 4.25 it is clearly seen that the 't' value 0.3481 between the mean values of awareness on Edusat and e-mail are Not Significantly Correlated and

0.4300, 0.4599 and 0.4799 between Edusat and Computer and Edusat and Internet and Edusat and Online device are Significantly Correlated at 0.05 level. Hence the framed Null hypothesis that there is no relationship between the Edusat and the other devices is accepted except Computers, Internet and Online devices.

Table 4.26. Significant Relationship in the Mean Scores of Awareness between e-mail and the Other ICT Devices

S.No.	Category	N	't' Value	Remarks
1.	e-mail-Computer	200	0.1758	NSC
2.	e-mail-Internet	200	0.2238	NSC
3.	e-mail-Edusat	200	0.3481	NSC
4.	e-mail-Online	200	0.5928	SC

On observing the table 10.26 it is obvious clear that the 't' values 0.1758, 0.2238 and 0.3481 between the mean values of awareness on e-mail and Computer and e-mail and Internet and e-mail and Edusat are Not Significantly Correlated and 0.5928 between e-mail and Online are Significantly Correlated at 0.05 level. Hence the framed Null hypothesis that there is no relationship between the e-mail and the other devices is accepted except online devices.

Table 10.27. Significant Relationship in the Mean Scores of Awareness between online and the Other ICT Devices

S.No.	Category	N	't' Value	Remarks
1.	Online—Computer	200	0.2468	NSC
2.	Online—Internet	200	0.3356	NSC
3.	Online—Edusat	200	0.4799	SC
4.	Online—e-mail	200	0.5928	SC

On observing the table 10.27 it is inferred that the 't' values 0.2468, 0.3356 between the mean values of awareness on Online and Computer and Online and Internet are Not Significantly Correlated and 0.4799 and 0.5928 between

Online and Edusat and Online and e-mail are Significantly Correlated at 0.05 level. Hence the framed Null hypothesis that there is no relationship between the Online devices and the other devices is accepted except Edusat and e-mail.

The forthcoming Chapter deals with the findings, discussion, suggestions for the further study, educational implications and conclusion of the study.

Findings and Conclusion

Chapter 11

INTRODUCTION

The purpose of the study was to measure the level of awareness on ICT devices among PG teachers with respect to Sex *i.e.* Male and Female, Locality of the PG teachers *i.e.* Urban and Rural, Type of the School *i.e.* Girls and Co-Education schools, Type of Management *i.e.* Government, Aided and Self-financing, Educational Qualification of the teachers *i.e.* P.G B.Ed., P.G.M.Ed., and PG M.Phil. Previous Knowledge in Computers *i.e.* Yes or No, the subjects taught by the teachers *i.e.* Arts and Science and finally the level of relationship between the various ICT devices among themselves in total. The study belongs to Normative Survey. The total samples selected for the study is 200 PG teachers working in Government, Aided and Self-financing Higher secondary schools of Tiruchirapalli District. The investigator developed an Awareness Questionnaire on ICT devices among the PG teachers and in which further classifications such as the awareness on Computers, Internet, Edusat, e-mail and Online devices were also considered. The data was collected from administering the Awareness Questionnaire among the PG teachers. The collected data was carefully processed and systematically analysed. Findings and conclusions were derived from the results from the *Chapter X*.

The present *chapter* deals with the Findings, Discussion and Conclusion, Educational Implications and Suggestion for the further study.

FINDINGS OF THE STUDY

The findings of the study are presented in the following eight sections.

Section A : Awareness on ICT Devices with Respect to Sex

- The mean scores of the awareness on ICT in total among the Male and Female PG teachers are similar.
- The mean scores of the awareness on Computers among the Male and Female PG teachers are similar.
- The mean scores of the awareness on Internet among the Male and Female PG teachers are similar.
- The mean scores of the awareness on Edusat among the Male and Female PG teachers are similar.
- The mean scores of the awareness on e-mail among the Female PG teachers were Significantly higher than the Male PG teachers.
- The mean scores of the awareness on Online devices among the Male and Female PG teachers are similar.

Section B : Awareness on ICT Devices with Respect to Locality

- The mean scores of the awareness on ICT in total among the Urban and Rural locality PG teachers are similar.
- The mean scores of the awareness on Computers among the Urban and Rural locality PG teachers are similar.
- The mean scores of the awareness on Internet among the Urban and Rural locality PG teachers are similar.

- The mean scores of the awareness on Edusat among the Urban and Rural locality PG teachers are similar.
- The mean scores of the awareness on e-mail among the Urban locality PG teachers were Significantly higher than the Rural locality PG teachers.
- The mean scores of the awareness on Online devices among the Urban locality PG teachers were Significantly higher than the Rural locality PG teachers.

Section C : Awareness on ICT Devices with Respect to Type of the School

- The mean scores of the awareness on ICT in total among the PG teachers of Girls and Co-education school are similar.
- The mean scores of the awareness on Computers in among the PG teachers of Girls and Co-education school are similar.
- The mean scores of the awareness on Internet among the PG teachers of Girls Schools were significantly lower than the Co-education school PG teachers.
- The mean scores of the awareness on Edusat among the PG teachers of Girls and Co-education school are similar.
- The mean scores of the awareness on e-mail among the PG teachers of Girls Schools were significantly higher than the Co-education school PG teachers.
- The mean scores of the awareness on online devices among the PG teachers of Girls Schools were significantly higher than the Co-education school PG teachers.

Section D : Awareness on ICT Devices with Respect to Management of the Schools

- The mean scores of the awareness on ICT in total among the PG teachers of Government and Aided schools are similar.

- The mean scores of the awareness on Computers among the PG teachers of Government and Aided schools are similar.
- The mean scores of the awareness on Internet among the PG teachers of Government and Aided schools are similar.
- The mean scores of the awareness on Edusat among the PG teachers of Government and Aided schools are similar.
- The mean scores of the awareness on e-mail among the PG teachers of Aided schools were Significantly higher than the Government school PG teachers.
- The mean scores of the awareness on Online devices among the PG teachers of Aided schools were Significantly higher than the Government school PG teachers.
- The mean scores of the awareness on ICT in total among the Aided and Self-financing school PG teachers are similar.
- The mean scores of the awareness Computers among the Aided and Self-financing school PG teachers are similar.
- The mean scores of awareness on Internet among the Self-financing school PG teachers were Significantly higher than the Aided school teachers.
- The mean scores of the awareness Edusat among the Aided and Self-financing school PG teachers are similar.
- The mean scores of the awareness e-mail among the Aided and Self-financing school PG teachers are similar.
- The mean scores of the awareness online devices among the Aided and Self-financing school PG teachers are similar.

- The mean scores of the awareness on ICT in total among the Government and Self-financing school PG teachers are similar.
- The mean scores of the awareness Computers among the Government and Self-financing school PG teachers are similar.
- The mean scores of awareness on Internet among the Self-financing school PG teachers were Significantly higher than the Government school teachers.
- The mean scores of the awareness Edusat among the Government and Self-financing school PG teachers are similar.
- The mean scores of the awareness e-mail among the Government and Self-financing school PG teachers are similar.
- The mean scores of the awareness online devices among the Government and Self-financing school PG teachers are similar.

Section E : Awareness on ICT Devices with Respect to Qualification

- The mean scores of the awareness on ICT in total among PG teachers whose qualifications are PG B.Ed. and PG M.Ed. are similar.
- The mean scores of the awareness on Computers among PG teachers whose qualifications are PG B.Ed. and PG M.Ed. are similar.
- The mean scores of the awareness on Internet among PG teachers whose qualifications are PG B.Ed. and PG M.Ed. are similar.
- The mean scores of the awareness on Edusat among PG teachers whose qualifications are PG B.Ed. and PG M.Ed. are similar.

- The mean scores of the awareness on e-mail among PG teachers whose qualifications are PG B.Ed. and PG M.Ed. are similar.
- The mean scores of the awareness on Online devices among PG teachers whose qualifications are PG B.Ed. and PG M. Ed. are similar.
- The mean scores of the awareness on ICT in total among PG teachers whose qualifications are PG M.Ed. and PG M. Phil. are similar.
- The mean scores of the awareness on Computers among PG teachers whose qualifications are PG M.Ed. and PG M. Phil. are similar.
- The mean scores of the awareness on Internet among PG teachers whose qualifications are PG M.Ed. and PG M. Phil. are similar.
- The mean scores of the awareness on Edusat among PG teachers whose qualifications are PG M.Ed. and PG M. Phil. are similar.
- The mean scores of the awareness on e-mail among PG teachers whose qualifications are PG M.Ed. and PG M. Phil. are similar.
- The mean scores of the awareness on Online devices among PG teachers whose qualifications are PG M.Ed. and PG M. Phil. are similar.
- The mean scores of the awareness on ICT in total among PG teachers whose qualifications are PG B.Ed. and PG M. Phil. are similar.
- The mean scores of the awareness on Computers among PG teachers whose qualifications are PG B.Ed. and PG M. Phil. are similar.
- The mean scores of the awareness on Internet among PG teachers whose qualifications are PG B.Ed. and PG M. Phil. are similar.
- The mean scores of the awareness on Edusat among PG teachers whose qualifications are PG B.Ed. and PG M.Phil. are similar.

- The mean scores of awareness on e-mail among the PG teachers whose qualifications are PG B.Ed is Significantly higher than the teachers of qualification PG M.Phil.
- The mean scores of the awareness on Online devices among PG teachers whose qualifications are PG B.Ed. and PG M.Phil. are similar.

Section F : Awareness on ICT Devices with Respect to Knowledge in Computers

- The mean scores of the awareness on ICT in total between the PG teachers those who have computer knowledge is Significantly higher than the teachers those who do not have computer knowledge.
- The mean scores of the awareness on Computers between the PG teachers those who have computer knowledge is Significantly higher than the teachers those who do not have computer knowledge.
- The mean scores of the awareness on Internet between the PG teachers those who have computer knowledge is Significantly higher than the teachers those who do not have computer knowledge.
- The mean scores of Awareness on Edusat among the PG teachers those who have and do not have computer knowledge are similar.
- The mean scores of Awareness on e-mail among the PG teachers those who have and do not have computer knowledge are similar.
- The mean scores of Awareness on Online devices among the PG teachers those who have and do not have computer knowledge are similar.

Section G : Awareness on ICT Devices with Respect to Subjects Taught by the Teachers

- The mean scores of the awareness on ICT in total between the PG teachers those who are teaching Arts and Science subjects are similar.

- The mean scores of the awareness on Computers between the PG teachers those who are teaching Arts and Science subjects are similar.
- The mean scores of the awareness on Internet between the PG teachers those who are teaching Arts and Science subjects are similar.
- The mean scores of the awareness on Edusat between the PG teachers those who are teaching Arts and Science subjects are similar.
- The mean scores of the awareness on e-mail between the PG teachers those who are teaching Arts and Science subjects are similar.
- The mean scores of the awareness on Online devices between the PG teachers those who are teaching Arts and Science subjects are similar.

Section H : Relationship in Awareness on ICT Devices among the PG Teachers in Total

- The mean scores of awareness on Computers and Internet among PG teachers in total were similar.
- The mean scores of awareness on Computers and Edusat among PG teachers in total were similar.
- The mean scores of awareness on Computers among PG teachers in total were lesser than the awareness on e-mail.
- The mean scores of awareness on Computers among PG teachers in total were higher than the awareness on Online devices.
- The mean scores of awareness on Internet among PG teachers in total were lesser than the awareness on Computers.
- The mean scores of awareness on Internet among PG teachers in total were lesser than the awareness on Edusat.

- The mean scores of awareness on Internet and e-mail among PG teachers in total were similar.
- The mean scores of awareness on Internet and Online devices among PG teachers in total were similar.
- The mean scores of awareness on Edusat among PG teachers in total were Significantly lower than the awareness on Computers.
- The mean scores of awareness on Edusat among PG teachers in total were Significantly higher than the awareness on Internet.
- The mean scores of awareness on Edusat and e-mail among the PG teachers in total were similar.
- The mean scores of awareness on Edusat among PG teachers in total were Significantly higher than the awareness on Online devices.
- The mean scores of awareness on e-mail and Computers among the PG teachers in total were similar.
- The mean scores of awareness on e-mail and Internet among the PG teachers in total were similar.
- The mean scores of awareness on e-mail and Edusat among the PG teachers in total were similar.
- The mean scores of awareness on e-mail among PG teachers in total were Significantly higher than the awareness on Online devices.
- The mean scores of awareness on Online devices and Computers among the PG teachers in total were similar.
- The mean scores of awareness on Online devices and Internet among the PG teachers in total were similar.
- The mean scores of awareness on Online devices among PG teachers in total were Significantly lesser than the awareness on Edusat.
- The mean scores of awareness on Online devices among PG teachers in total were Significantly lesser than the awareness on e-mail.

DISCUSSION OF THE STUDY

The mean scores of the awareness on e-mail among female P.G teachers were Significantly higher than the male P.G teachers. This may be due to the curiosity of lady teachers. Women are naturally duty-oriented, sincere and faithful so they use e-mail regularly.

The mean scores of awareness on e-mail and online devices among urban locality P.G teachers are Significantly higher than rural locality P.G teachers the urban locality P.G teachers may have various e-mail and online facilities like browsing centers, web sites etc., It is easy to reach them. On the other hand, rural P.G teachers must spend time, money to reach browsing centers. The urban P.G teachers can spend even night time at browsing centers but teachers in rural area cannot spend time as there are no proper transport facilities.

The means scores of awareness on e-mail and online devices among P.G teachers of aided schools were Significantly higher than government school P.G teachers this is because the management helps them a lot.

The mean scores of awareness on Internet among self-financing schools P.G teachers are significantly higher than Aided schools and Government schools P.G teachers. The self-financing infrastructure is good, up to date modern. Internet facilities are available to them.

EDUCATIONAL IMPLICATIONS

Teachers working in government schools and Aided Schools must be considered for acquiring more awareness towards ICT's. Hence the policy makers should organise in-service training programme to develop confidence among P.G teachers in using ICT's as instructional tools.

As the Aided schools P.G teachers having Significantly more awareness towards ICT's they may be encouraged more to use software in classroom instructions. All the P.G teachers may be encouraged by giving apparent training on preparing CAI software with more interaction.

SUGGESTIONS FOR THE FUTUTRE RESEARCH

- The study may be conducted in all the other districts of Tamilnadu with the variables such as Locality, Sex, Type of School, Educational Qualification and the Previous Knowledge in Computers.
- The study may be conducted among PG Teachers of Higher Secondary Schools in Metropolitan cities.
- The study may also conduct among all the teachers such as SGTT, BT Teachers of Government, Aided and Self-financing High and Higher Secondary schools.
- The study may be conducted among PG Teachers related to the classifications of ICT devices other than, the awareness on Computers, Internet, and Edusat, e-mail and Online devices also.

LIMITATIONS OF THE STUDY

- The time at the disposal of the investigator for the study is rather short.
- The study is limited to a sample of 200 PG Teachers only.
- The sample is confined to the area of Tiruchirapalli District with the limited variables such as Locality, Sex, Type of School, Educational Qualification and the Previous Knowledge in Computers.
- The study is confined only to PG Teachers of Government, Aided and Self-financing Higher secondary schools
- The study is related to the classifications of ICT devices such as the awareness on Computers, Internet, Edusat, e-mail and Online devices only.
- The investigator found a limited research studies, journals on the selected exact topics.

CONCLUSION

From the findings it could be concluded that P.G teachers were having positive awareness towards the use of ICT's in educations. From test of significance of mean scores it is concluded that teachers in urban locality working in Aided schools are more aware of using Online and e-mail than teachers of rural locality. Investigation also reveals that awareness on Internet is found more among P.G teachers of self-financing institutions than P.G teachers of Aided Schools and government schools

REFERENCES

1. Almekhlafi Abdurrahman Ghalab (2005) Preserves Teachers Attitude Perceptions of the Utility of Web-based Instructions in the United Arab Emirates *International Journal of the United Arab Emirates* Internal Journal of Instructional Media, 32(3).
2. Bailey, Terry D (1990) The Superintendent's Perception of the Instructional Technology in Virginia School Division.
3. Bond-Upson, Deborah; Latham, Andrew; Bartone, Linda (2000) School Planning and Management, Suppl.
4. Bruning, Stephen D (1995) Classroom Exercise That Incorporates Internet Discussion Groups as an Integral Element in a Communication Course.
5. Carter, D. S. G.; Leah, D. J. K. (2001) Validating Behavioural Changes: Teachers' Perception and Use of ICT in England and Korea.
6. Chandra, Peter (1987) How Do Teachers View Their Teaching and Use of Teaching Resources? *British Journal of Education Technology,* 18 (2).
7. Chen, Tzy-Ling; Chen, Tzu-Jump (2006) Examination of Attitude Towards Teaching Online Courses Based on Theory of Reasoned Action of University *Faculty in Taiwan British Journal of Educational Technology,* 37 (5).
8. Da Ponte, Joao Pedro; Oliveira, Varandas, Joes Manuel (2002). Development of Preservice Mathematics Teachers' Professional Knowledge and Identity in Working with Information and Communication Technology *Journal of Mathematics Teacher Education,* 5 (2).
9. Di, Xu; Dunn, Denise; Lee, S. J (2000) An Integrated to Instructional Technology. *Action in Teacher Education,* 22 (2A).

10. Diusick, Diane M. (1999) Effect of Administrative Support Policies, Cognitive Processes and Motivational Beliefs on Faculty Uses Computer Technology; Testing a Motivational Model.

11. Friedman, Adam (2006) K-12 Teachers; Use of Course Websites Journal of Technology and Teachers Education, 14 (4).

12. Gray, Carol (1996) Will Your NQT Use IT? Language Journal, (13).

13. Gurbuz, Tarkan; Yildirim, I. Soner; Ozden, M. Yasar (2000) A Comparison of Student Teachers' Aptitudes Towards Computers in Online and Traditional Computer Literacy Courses: A Case Study http://www.tect.unt.edu/research/survey/tat32a.pdf

14. Ivers, Karen S (2001) *Educational Technology Professional Development Programme*.

15. Ivers, Karen S.; Barron, Ann E. (1997) Training for Telecommunications: Examining the Effects of Video and Computer-based Instruction on Preservice Teachers' Achievement, Near-Transfer Performance, and Perception of Instruction. *Journal of Computing in Teacher Education,* 13 (3).

16. Jennings, Miranda E.; Holcomb, Lori B.; Lima, Clarisse O.; Brown, Scott W. (2005) Teachers' Perception of Their Classroom Technological Resources and the Perceived Feasibility of Implementation of Their Connecticut Teacher Technology Competencies: Level II Proposals. Online Submission, *paper presented at Annual Meeting of the Northeastern Educational Research Association* (Kerhonkson) NY, Oct 20.

17. Jack Pillemer (1997) e-mail as a Teaching Tool http://www.etni.org.il/jack.htm

18. Kenn Martin, (1999) Why Use e-mail in Your Teaching? *Issues of Teaching and Learning* 5(3).

19. Kenn Martin, (1999) Advantages and Disadvantages in Using E-mail for Teaching and Learning 5(3).

20. Knezek, G. and Christensen, R. (1998). Internal Consistency Reliability for the Teachers' Attitude towards Information Technology and Questionnaire. Presented at Society of Information Technology and Teacher Education (SITE)'s 5th International Conference, Washington, DC, and March 13, 1998. In http://tect.unt.edu/reseach/sitetat/sld001.htm

21. Kollias, V.; Mamalougos, N.; Vamvakoussi, X.; lakala, M.; Vosniadou, S (2005) Teachers' Attitudes to and Beliefs About Web-based Collaborative Learning Environments in the Context of an International Implementation Computers and Education, 45 (3).

22. MacNeil, Angus J.; Delafield, Dennis P. (1998). *Principal Leadership for Successful School Technology Implementation.*

23. Madden Andrew; Ford, Nigel; Miller, David; Levy, Philippa (2005). Using the Internet in Teaching: The Views of Practitioners (A Survey of the Secondary School Teachers in Sheffield, UK) *British journal of Educational Technology, 36 (2).*

24. Mitra, Ananda (1994) "Instructor-effect" in Determining Effectiveness and Attitude Towards Technology-assisted Teaching: Report of a *Case Study. Journal of Instruction Delivery Systems.* 8 (3).

25. Narasimha Bolloju, Learning Through Asynchronous Discussions Dept of Information System, City University of Hong Kong, and Robert Division,, Dept of Information System, City University of Hong Kong in http://www.elearmag.org subpage.cfm?section= tutorials&article=12-1.

26. Norby, Rena Faye (2003) It Is a Gender Issue! Change in Attitude Towards Science in a Technology based K-8 Pre-service Preparation Science Classroom.

27. Smith, Irene Elizabeth (1993) An Investigation into Students' Perceptions of the Learning Environment Provided by Hypermedia Tools in an Interdisciplinary High School Course of Studies.

28. Tu, chih-hsiung (2000) Strategies to Increase Interaction in Online Social Learning Environments.

29. Vinary Kumar, Julia Bedell, Vernon Hicks, Allen H.Seed, (2000) Proceedings of Society for *Information Technology and Teacher Education International Conference.*

30. Wang, Yu-me (1996) e-mail Dialogue Journaling in an ESL Reading and Writing Classroom.

31. Wang, Yu-mei; Cohen, Ariene (1998) University Faculty—Use of the Internet.

32. Wedman, John F (1986) Educational Computing In Service Design: Implications from Teachers' Concerns Research.

33. Yang, H., Jong, Y, & Chao, S. (2002). A Study of Technology Teachers' Attitude Towards Video-conference Applied in Education. In C. Crawford *et al.* (Eds.), Proceedings of Sociality for Information Technology and Teacher Educational Conference 2002 (pp.2349-2350). Chesapeake, VA: AACE.

Index